TANKMASTER

A practical guide to creating and maintaining
WATER QUALITY

PETER HISCOCK

BARRON'S

Author

Peter Hiscock began keeping fish and aquariums as a child, inspired by his parents, both accomplished marine biologists. He was appointed manager of a retail aquatics outlet at just 17 years of age and went on to complete aquatic studies at Sparsholt College in Hampshire, UK. He entered publishing with contributions to the aquatic press. His main interests include fish behavior and the interaction of fish with their environment, as well as aquascaping and the natural habitats of aquarium species.

First edition for the United States and Canada published by Barron's Educational Series, Inc., 2001
First published in 2000 by Interpet Publishing
Original edition © 2000 by Interpet Publishing

All inquiries should be addressed to:
Barron's Educational Series, Inc.
250 Wireless Boulevard
Hauppauge, NY 11788
http://www.barronseduc.com

International Standard Book No. 0-7641-5274-2
Library of Congress Catalog Card No. 00-109057

Printed in China
9 8 7 6 5 4 3 2 1

Credits
Created and designed:
Ideas into Print,
New Ash Green, Kent DA3 8JD,
England.

Below: The author diving at Likoma Island, Lake Malawi. The scene is typical of the clear, alkaline waters of the lake, where the Malawi cichlids have adapted and evolved to survive in this environment.

Contents

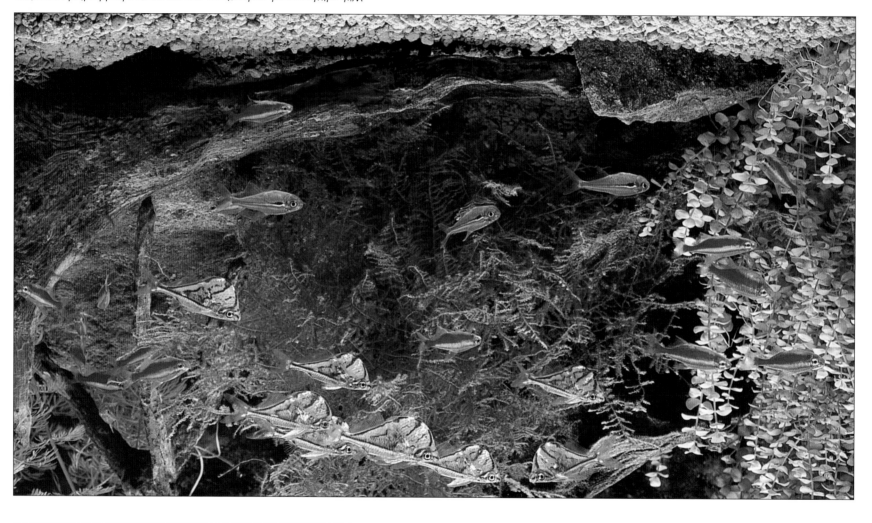

Providing the correct environment

Most popular pets are domesticated animals and, given the correct care, are quite happy in an environment that is far removed from the natural habitat of their wild ancestors. With fish, the story is different; each species has evolved to survive in its natural habitat and in most cases cannot be considered domesticated. This means that to thrive in the aquarium, fish must be housed in conditions that are as close as possible to their natural environment. A fish's direct environment – water – is a very dynamic one; in nature and in the aquarium there are many continuous biological and chemical processes that constantly change and shape the qualities of the water. Although these processes cannot often be seen, it is the job of the fishkeeper to monitor water quality and ensure that the whole aquarium environment is working as it should be, both biologically and chemically. Water quality affects a fish's body directly.

Species from naturally soft and acidic waters have the necessary physical adaptations to live in these waters and will not do well in hard, alkaline water. Conversely, fish from hard, alkaline water will not survive well in soft, acidic water. To achieve the best conditions in the aquarium, we must look at the processes that occur in nature and understand how the natural environment is formed. To be successful as fishkeepers, we have to provide an environment in which the fish we keep will be able to live healthily. If the conditions are not right, the aquarium will not thrive and the fish will suffer. Virtually all the problems encountered by new fishkeepers boil down to poor environmental conditions caused directly or indirectly by the fishkeeper. By taking a little time beforehand to ensure that conditions are as good as they can be, you will be able to avoid many setbacks and enjoy your hobby with minimal problems.

THE NATURAL WATER CYCLE

In nature, water is continually moving and changing. The hydrological cycle shown below follows the natural movement of water as it travels from the atmosphere, through lakes, rivers, and oceans, and then back into the atmosphere. Although there is no beginning to this cycle, it makes sense to start with the evaporation and transpiration of water caused by heat and radiation from the sun.

The sun as a water pump

The heat of the sun causes evaporation from any water surface, most importantly from the oceans. Water vapor is also lost through the leaves of plants, a process called transpiration. The combined process, called evapotranspiration, describes the movement of water as vapor into the atmosphere. At higher altitudes, changes in air pressure and temperature cause the water vapor to condense into clouds. As they move over the land and pressures change, clouds may become denser and more concentrated with water vapor. Eventually, they become so dense that the vapor turns into droplets of water that then fall as rain.

Pure, but not for long

Evaporated water is pure and contains no contaminants, but as soon as water droplets are formed and begin to fall through the atmosphere, they pick up substances that change their chemical makeup. Initially, oxygen and carbon dioxide are picked up from the air, followed by dust particles and airborne pollutants. Carbon dioxide and water produce carbonic acid, so most rainfall is slightly acidic by the time it reaches the ground. One common airborne pollutant is sulphur dioxide, produced by factories and power stations. It causes rain to become so acid ("acid rain") that it may be damaging to vegetation and living organisms.

Fallen rain can take a number of routes. Initial run-off occurs when the water simply flows over the surface and collects in streams and rivers. Some water soaks into the topsoil and is held in place by the roots of plants. Excess water flows through the soil and, again, ends up in streams and rivers.

Flowing across the land in rivers, streams, and as runoff, water will pick up organic compounds from vegetation (which create soft, acidic water) and carbonates and minerals from rock (which cause it to become hard and alkaline). Over agricultural land, water may pick up organic pollutants from the soil, including pesticides, herbicides, fertilizers, and organophosphates, which may cause high levels of nitrogenous and phosphorous compounds. Water from agricultural runoff is often green with the algae that thrive in these conditions, but may be toxic to many forms of aquatic life, including fish. There is normally enough water in rivers to dilute pollutants to levels low enough to cause minimal problems.

The underground route

If the rainfall continues, the ground becomes waterlogged and water percolates down through the topsoil until it reaches underground rocks. Depending on the type of rock, the water is slowly absorbed and travels down through the earth. As it permeates the rock, it picks up mineral compounds and

Above: Pure, unpolluted water collects in the skies, preparing to fall as rain. When it reaches the ground, it has a long journey to make before it finally reaches the oceans.

becomes hard and alkaline. Some of this water will remain deep underground and may form underground pools. This often happens when a soluble and easily eroded rock meets a harder, impenetrable rock below, and the water remains between the two. Once underground, the water may reach the surface again by way of springs, or it may travel to lower land through underground streams.

On the beach

Finally, the water reaches the oceans. As we have seen, at this point it is often high in organic material and minerals, and also carries sediment in suspension that is deposited at the mouth of the river. In fact, the ocean's salt content has built up over millions of years from the erosion of rock and the minerals carried in from rivers.

How water circulates and is modified on the way

Rainfall
As it falls, rainwater begins to change. Pollutants and airborne chemicals are picked up on the way down, making the water slightly acidic.

Condensation
As warm moist air rises, it cools and the water vapor condenses onto tiny airborne particles to form clouds of water droplets that grow into raindrops.

Evapotranspiration
Water evaporates from rivers, lakes, and oceans and transpires from trees and vegetation. Only pure water passes into the air, leaving any chemicals behind.

Surface runoff
As the water reaches the ground, it flows through and over the topsoil. Humic acids and carbon dioxide make it more acidic and minerals give the water hardness.

Percolation
Water percolating through rocks picks up nutrients and minerals. If it reaches an impermeable layer, it collects underground and emerges as a natural spring.

THE UNSEEN QUALITIES OF WATER

Pure water (H₂O) very rarely, if ever, occurs in nature and if it did, it would not be suitable for fish to live in. Minerals, salts, and organic matter all affect water chemistry, and fish prefer different "types" of water, depending on where they originate in nature. This summary of water characteristics forms an introduction to the sections that follow, where each parameter is examined in more detail.

H₂O

Oxygen

Hydrogen

WATER
Pure water molecules are made up of two hydrogen atoms and one oxygen atom bound together. It is the additional chemicals and environmental factors that create specific conditions within water.

Oxygen (O_2)
All living organisms need oxygen for respiration (breathing) and energy production. In the aquarium, oxygen is used up by fish, bacteria, and plants and is replenished by diffusion through the water surface. Surface agitation increases the air/water exchange and allows more oxygen to enter the water. Through photosynthesis, plants produce more oxygen in daylight than they use up.

Carbon dioxide (CO_2)
Carbon dioxide is a waste product of respiration in plants and animals. It is regulated in the aquarium through the air/water exchange at the surface. Carbon dioxide can be artificially introduced to the aquarium for use as a plant fertilizer and to regulate pH levels.

Hardness
Water can be described as hard or soft, depending on the amount of dissolved calcium and magnesium salts it contains. The most widely used scale to measure hardness is degrees of hardness (°dGH). Some fish prefer hard water, with a high concentration of salts, while others prefer soft water with a low salt concentration.

Temperature
Most tropical fish live happily at temperatures between 24 and 27°C (75-80°F). Temperature can affect oxygen levels and the toxicity of some pollutants in the aquarium.

Salinity
Salinity is an overall measure of the dissolved salt content of water. Seawater has a salt content of 35ppt (parts per thousand). Fresh water has a salinity of no more than 1ppt.

Acidity and alkalinity (pH)

The degree of acidity or alkalinity of water is measured on the pH scale. This runs from 0 (extremely acid) to 14 (extremely alkaline), with pH 7 representing the neutral point. Tropical freshwater fish can be found in water with pH levels of 4–9, although the majority are found between 6 and 8.5.

Chlorine (Cl_2)

Chlorine gas is added to tap water to kill harmful bacteria and make it safe for human consumption. Chlorine is toxic to fish and can damage filtration systems, so it is vital to remove it by adding a dechlorinating chemical or by aerating the tap water before using it in the aquarium.

Chloramine

When chlorine is mixed with nitrogenous compounds, chloramine is created. Chloramine is not toxic to fish, but it releases toxic chlorine over time. Chloramine can be removed from tap water by using a dechlorinator.

Specific gravity

This is another way of measuring salt content. Water with a high amount of salt becomes denser and its specific gravity rises. Pure water has a specific gravity of 1 and seawater has a specific gravity between 1.021 and 1.024.

Ammonia (NH_3)

Ammonia is a highly toxic substance produced from the breakdown of food and found in fish waste. Ammonia can be removed by biological or chemical filtration. It is also known as "free ammonia."

Ammonium (NH_4^+)

This is not as toxic as free ammonia. The balance of ammonia and ammonium is altered by pH and temperature levels.

Nitrite (NO_2)

Ammonia is converted into nitrite by bacteria that grow in colonies on the gravel and in biological filters. Nitrite is not as toxic as ammonia, but it is still highly dangerous to fish.

Nitrate (NO_3)

Nitrite is converted into nitrate by different kinds of bacteria that colonize the gravel and biological filter media. Nitrate is only dangerous to fish at high levels and usually can be kept in control by regular water changes.

All living organisms respire, or breathe, and need oxygen to do this. Fish use their gills to extract oxygen from the water (see fish physiology, page 50) and if too little oxygen is available or the fish is unable to extract enough oxygen, then its health will be adversely affected. Oxygen enters the water by diffusion at the water surface – the air/water interface. If the surface is agitated or constantly moving, then the air/water interface is increased and oxygen will enter the water more readily.

The amount of oxygen in the water reduces as a result of respiration by living organisms such as fish and plants. However, bacteria also use large amounts of oxygen to break down waste organic matter. If there is a great deal of organic matter in the aquarium, then bacteria can reduce the available oxygen to dangerously low levels. The amount of oxygen fish require depends on the type of fish. Larger, more active fish require higher oxygen levels. Some species can breathe atmospheric air, so oxygen levels in the water are less important to them.

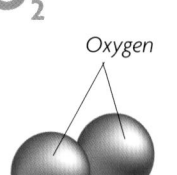

OXYGEN
In its most useful form, oxygen is found as two oxygen atoms bonded together. Oxygen gas makes up about 20 percent of the air. Almost all living organisms need oxygen to survive.

Oxygen

Oxygen levels also decrease as the temperature rises. This sometimes causes problems in the summer, especially in ponds. Here, the higher temperature usually coincides with an increased organic load and a bloom in plant or algae growth, all of which combine to reduce oxygen levels.

Plant respiration and photosynthesis
Plants are often bought for the aquarium for the purpose of introducing oxygen. Some plants have even been labeled collectively as "oxygenators," but it is important to understand exactly how plants produce oxygen. Plants photosynthesize during periods of daylight, using sunlight as a source of energy. A by-product of this process is the production of oxygen. Plants also respire, which involves the use of oxygen, although the oxygen produced by photosynthesis is greater than the amount used for respiration. However, photosynthesis stops at night while respiration continues, with the result that oxygen is taken from the water and not replaced. If a pond or aquarium is heavily planted and surface water movement is minimal, then oxygen concentration can fall to low levels during periods of darkness.

Oversaturation
It is possible to have too much oxygen in the water, which can also be highly dangerous to fish. Water has a saturation level that varies with temperature. The saturation level is the maximum amount of dissolved oxygen that the water can hold. Water may become oversaturated, or "supersaturated," by heavy

photosynthesis as a result of dense planting and high light levels, or by algal blooms. When this happens, the fishes' blood also becomes supersaturated. In supersaturated water, oxygen is quickly released from the water and small air bubbles are produced. This can also happen in the fishes' blood. Blisters may form beneath the skin and in the head and eyes, with potentially fatal results. To remedy the situation, install sufficient aeration. This helps the exchange of gas at the water surface, so it releases oxygen from the water, as well as introducing it.

Above: *Oxygen enters the water through the surface. If the surface area is greatly increased by agitation from a pump or filter, more oxygen can enter (or leave) the water.*

Oxygen in the aquarium

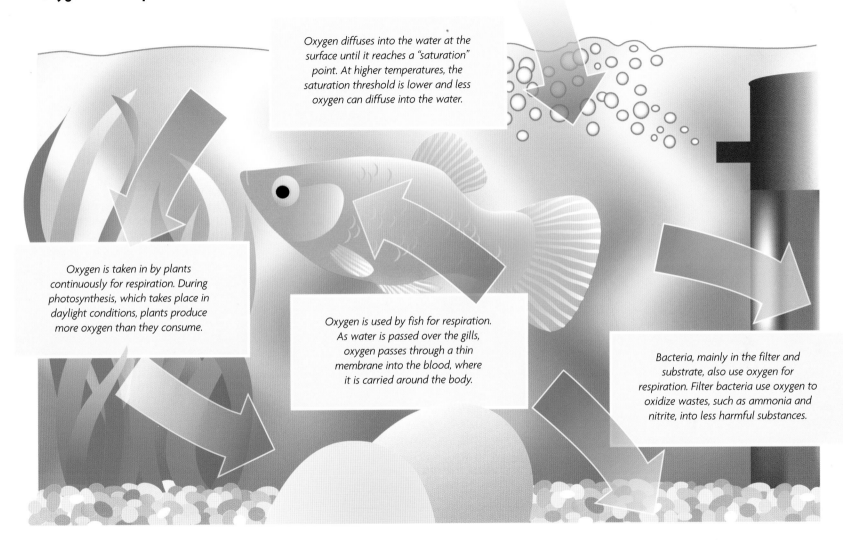

Oxygen diffuses into the water at the surface until it reaches a "saturation" point. At higher temperatures, the saturation threshold is lower and less oxygen can diffuse into the water.

Oxygen is taken in by plants continuously for respiration. During photosynthesis, which takes place in daylight conditions, plants produce more oxygen than they consume.

Oxygen is used by fish for respiration. As water is passed over the gills, oxygen passes through a thin membrane into the blood, where it is carried around the body.

Bacteria, mainly in the filter and substrate, also use oxygen for respiration. Filter bacteria use oxygen to oxidize wastes, such as ammonia and nitrite, into less harmful substances.

CARBON DIOXIDE

As oxygen is used up by respiration, so carbon dioxide (CO_2) is produced as a by-product. It is important in the aquarium for healthy plant growth. Plants use carbon dioxide for photosynthesis and without it healthy growth is impaired. In fact, carbon dioxide is often deliberately introduced to the aquarium as a plant fertilizer. Carbon dioxide in water produces carbonic acid, which can lower pH levels; removing carbon dioxide can increase pH levels. Carbon dioxide is used in this way to control pH levels in the aquarium. Providing that oxygen levels in the aquarium are sufficiently high for plant and animal respiration, then CO_2 levels are not overly important in most aquariums unless you are focusing more attention on plant growth. High surface agitation will remove CO_2 from the aquarium, so avoid this in planted tanks.

It is possible to have too much CO_2 in the aquarium, however. If this happens, the fish will exhibit similar symptoms to oxygen depletion, such as fast breathing, gasping at the surface, and jumping.

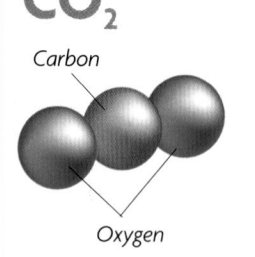

CO₂

CARBON DIOXIDE
Carbon
Oxygen

Carbon dioxide is a gas made up of one carbon atom bonded to two oxygen atoms. When carbon dioxide binds with water, carbonic acid (H_2CO_3) is produced.

Carbon dioxide and photosynthesis

Plants have special cells called chloroplasts that are able to use energy from light to combine water (H_2O) and carbon dioxide (CO_2) into glucose ($C_6H_{12}O_6$), producing oxygen as a waste product.

■ Oxygen

▨ Carbon dioxide

DAY

NIGHT

RESPIRATION

RESPIRATION

PHOTOSYNTHESIS

NO PHOTOSYNTHESIS

During the day, plants photosynthesize, using up carbon dioxide and producing oxygen. Plants also respire, using less oxygen than produced in photosynthesis and giving out less carbon dioxide than used up in photosynthesis.

At night, plants cannot photosynthesize due to the absence of light energy, but they continue to respire. At this time, both plants and fish are using up oxygen for respiration and producing carbon dioxide in the process.

Carbon dioxide in the aquarium

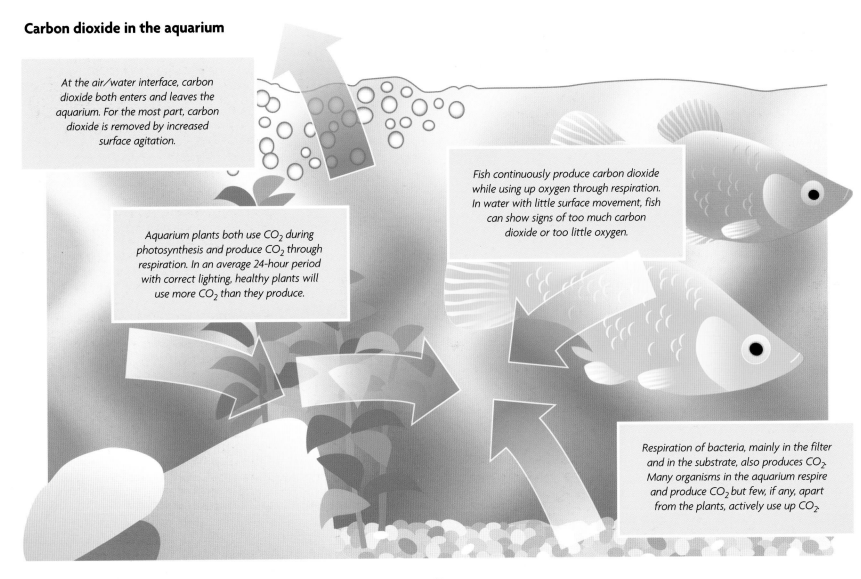

At the air/water interface, carbon dioxide both enters and leaves the aquarium. For the most part, carbon dioxide is removed by increased surface agitation.

Aquarium plants both use CO_2 during photosynthesis and produce CO_2 through respiration. In an average 24-hour period with correct lighting, healthy plants will use more CO_2 than they produce.

Fish continuously produce carbon dioxide while using up oxygen through respiration. In water with little surface movement, fish can show signs of too much carbon dioxide or too little oxygen.

Respiration of bacteria, mainly in the filter and in the substrate, also produces CO_2. Many organisms in the aquarium respire and produce CO_2 but few, if any, apart from the plants, actively use up CO_2.

CHLORINE

Chlorine is extremely toxic to all fish and is present in tap water at levels high enough to be considered dangerous to aquatic life. Chlorine is present in tap water for the benefit of people, as it destroys bacteria and other organic pollutants that would otherwise make tap water unsuitable for drinking. In the aquarium, fish depend on the bacteria in filters to carry out a waste disposal function. If these bacteria are not present or are killed by chlorine, then pollutants, such as ammonia and nitrites, will build up to toxic levels and eventually kill the fish. If the lack of filtration does not harm fish, then direct exposure to chlorine in the aquarium at high enough levels will. Tap water commonly contains between 0.2 and 0.5mg/liter of chlorine; for most fish these levels are lethal.

Thankfully, chlorine is relatively easy to remove from tap water before it is used in the aquarium. The easiest and most common method is to use a brand-name dechlorinator, which can be mixed with tap water to remove chlorine in a matter of minutes. The dechlorinated water is then safe to use in the aquarium, providing it is at the right temperature. Alternatively, leave a container of tap water to stand for 24 hours and aerate it to remove the chlorine, which will dissipate into the atmosphere. Chlorine also appears in a slightly different form – chloramine – which will release chlorine over a period of time. Not all dechlorinators remove chloramine, so check the label carefully.

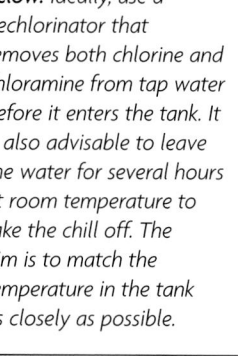

Below: Ideally, use a dechlorinator that removes both chlorine and chloramine from tap water before it enters the tank. It is also advisable to leave the water for several hours at room temperature to take the chill off. The aim is to match the temperature in the tank as closely as possible.

The effects of high chlorine levels on fish

High levels of chlorine, such as those found in tap water, can cause the following symptoms: shimmying, loss of color, reduced respiration, gill damage, death.

Cl₂

Chlorine

CHLORINE

Chlorine is a highly reactive and poisonous gas. When chlorine is added to water, it breaks up into various components. Some pure chlorine (Cl_2) remains, but most is broken up into chlorine ions (Cl^-), hydrogen ions (H^+), and hypochlorous acid ($HOCl$). It is the hypochlorous acid that damages fish and the beneficial filter bacteria. Because chlorine is introduced as a gas, it is relatively unstable; aeration, low pH, and high temperatures all help to remove or reduce chlorine and/or hypochlorous acid levels in the aquarium. Due to chlorine's instability, it is often mixed with nitrogenous compounds, such as ammonia, to create chloramine, which is much more stable and releases hypochlorous acid at a slower rate and in a more concentrated way.

Cleaning filters

Never clean filter media in tap water, as the chlorine will kill the useful bacteria. Always use water from the aquarium.

AMMONIA

Ammonia (NH_3) is mainly produced through decaying organic matter and fish waste, and is incredibly toxic to fish and other aquatic life. Ammonia levels of more than 0.02mg/liter can be toxic to fish over longer periods, while higher levels (0.2mg/liter or more) can kill within hours. Ideally, ammonia levels should be kept at zero at all times. In the aquarium, ammonia can easily change into ammonium (NH_4^+), which is far less toxic. To distinguish between the two forms, toxic ammonia is described as "free ammonia." The pH level of the water affects this change; at low pH levels, ammonia is more likely to appear as less toxic ammonium. This means that ammonia levels are more toxic in water with a high pH level.

Temperature also affects ammonia toxicity; higher temperatures cause more free ammonia to be released into the water. Test kits usually measure total ammonia levels (both ammonium and free ammonia), so it is often hard to measure how toxic the level of ammonia is in a sample of water.

NH_3

AMMONIA
The ammonia molecule is made up of three hydrogen atoms and one nitrogen atom. Bacteria convert ammonia through oxidation, replacing the hydrogen atoms with oxygen, to produce NO_2 and NO_3.

Hydrogen

Nitrogen

Testing for ammonia

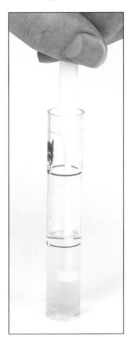

1 Ammonia should be tested for regularly, especially in new aquariums. This test kit uses tablets, which need to be crushed in a glass tube with the correct amount of water.

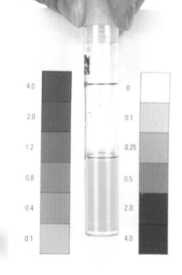

2 After a set period of time, the water in the tube can be compared with a color chart to obtain an ammonia reading. This water sample shows an ammonia level of 0.1mg/liter.

4.0	0
2.0	0.1
1.2	0.25
0.8	0.5
0.4	2.0
0.1	4.0

The causes of high ammonia levels

Dead fish, breakdown of filtration, introducing too many fish at once, too much dead organic matter.

The effects of high ammonia levels on fish

Gill damage, breathing difficulties, destruction of the mucus layer, internal and external bleeding, disease, erratic swimming and jumping (escape response), death.

How to reduce high ammonia levels

If levels of ammonia become dangerously high, carry out a series of water changes (no more than 30 percent each day) and use a proprietary ammonia remover. In serious cases, it may be worth changing all the aquarium water and replacing it with fresh, heated, and dechlorinated water.

NITRITE

Ammonia is converted into nitrite (NO_2) by *Nitrosomonas* spp. bacteria as part of the nitrogen cycle that takes place in the filter system (see page 20). Nitrite is less toxic than ammonia, but still dangerous and even deadly in the aquarium. Again, ideal levels should be zero.

Nitrite may occur for short periods when new fish are introduced or when the aquarium is new. (For more information, see the section on maturing the aquarium, page 34.) Lethal levels of nitrite vary according to the species of fish, but generally, levels of about 0.2mg/liter can be deadly. Symptoms of nitrite poisoning include listlessness and breathing problems.

Nitrite toleration

Nitrite breaks down red blood cells and oxidizes iron in the blood, changing hemoglobin into methemoglobin, which has no capacity to carry oxygen. Fish can change methemoglobin back into hemoglobin, but their ability to do this varies according to species, which is why some fish will tolerate much higher levels of nitrites than others.

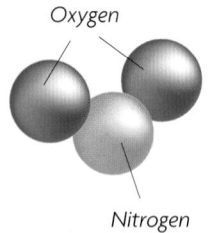

NO$_2$

Oxygen

Nitrogen

NITRITE

Nitrite consists of two oxygen atoms and one nitrogen atom. In the aquarium, nitrite often occurs as nitrous acid (HNO_2) when bonded with hydrogen, and forms similar compounds with potassium (KNO_2) and sodium ($NaNO_2$).

Testing for nitrite

Nitrite can occur briefly in a new aquarium. Regular testing is vital to ensure a healthy environment.

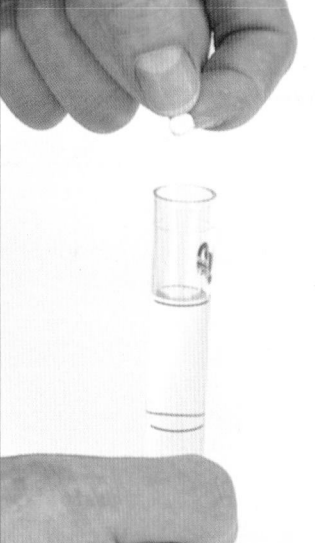

1 In this test kit, a single tablet is used in 10ml of aquarium water in a glass tube. It is vital to keep your hands clean and free from any chemicals that may affect the test.

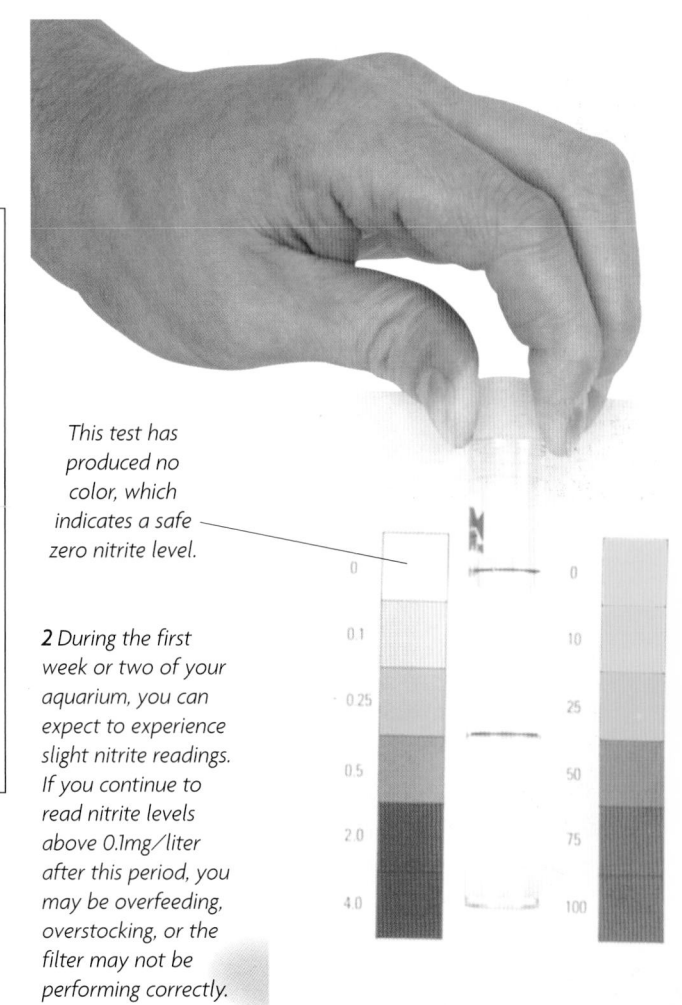

This test has produced no color, which indicates a safe zero nitrite level.

2 During the first week or two of your aquarium, you can expect to experience slight nitrite readings. If you continue to read nitrite levels above 0.1mg/liter after this period, you may be overfeeding, overstocking, or the filter may not be performing correctly.

NITRATE

Just as ammonia is converted into nitrites by *Nitrosomonas* spp. bacteria, so nitrites are converted into nitrates (NO_3) by *Nitrobacter* spp. bacteria. Nitrates are far less toxic than either ammonia or nitrites, but can cause damage to fish if levels are allowed to rise too high. In most fish, lethal levels can vary from 50 to 250mg/liter, but many fish can tolerate much higher levels. High nitrate levels are most likely to damage fish indirectly, by lowering their natural immunity as a result of stress and allowing disease to appear. Nitrate is not removed from the aquarium by normal filtration processes and will build up over time. The best way of controlling nitrate levels is to do regular water changes, thereby reducing nitrates by dilution. Some tap water contains nitrates, so it may be hard, if not impossible, to eliminate them altogether. Activated carbon cannot remove NO_2 or any other ionic solute from the aquarium water. Zeolites or other ion exchangers are necessary for this.

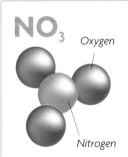

NO₃

Oxygen

Nitrogen

NITRATE
Almost identical to nitrite, but with the addition of an extra oxygen atom, nitrate usually occurs as salts of nitric acid (HNO_3), such as potassium nitrate (KNO_3) and sodium nitrate ($NaNO_3$). The test is simply for nitrate.

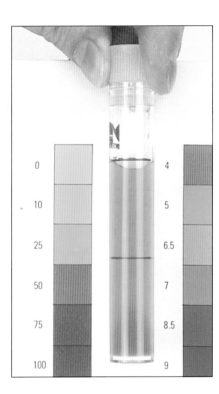

Above: This nitrate test shows a mid-range reading, which is harmless to most hardy fish, but may cause longer-term problems if left unchecked. If you find nitrate readings gradually rising, you may need to increase the frequency of water changes, introduce some live plants, or occasionally use a chemical filter medium to reduce levels.

Anaerobic bacteria and nitrate levels

In some aquariums, especially those designed for plants, areas of little or no oxygen form in the substrate. In these areas, anaerobic bacteria carry out a process called denitrification.

During denitrification, oxygen is stripped away from nitrogenous compounds such as nitrate, leaving nitrogen gas, which is released into the water, thus reducing nitrate levels.

Below: *Nitrates are a good source of nutrients for plants. In a planted aquarium such as this, healthy plants will keep nitrate levels to a minimum.*

The nitrogen cycle is a biological process that involves the continual circulation of nitrogenous compounds such as ammonia, nitrite, and nitrate. These are the main biological toxins found in the aquarium, so it is important that the nitrogen cycle works effectively to remove these pollutants. The reason for stocking new aquariums slowly, and taking time to mature them, is to allow the nitrogen cycle to develop and keep pace with the gradual increase of waste matter. If overfeeding occurs and too many fish are introduced too quickly, the bacteria that form a vital part of the nitrogen cycle will not be sufficiently developed to cope with the influx of waste, and ammonia and nitrites will build up to lethal levels.

AMMONIA
Ammonia comes not only from fish excreta, but also from any decomposing biological matter, such as uneaten food or dead plant leaves. Ammonia is highly toxic to aquatic life and must be quickly removed or converted.

NH_3

BACTERIAL CONVERSION
Nitrosomonas spp. bacteria carry out the first conversion of a nitrogenous compound (in effect, the first stage of biological filtration). Through the addition of an oxygen molecule, they convert ammonia (NH_3) into nitrite (NO_2).

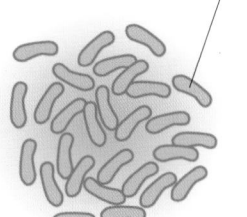

BREAKDOWN OF PROTEINS
Fish food contains 30–60 percent protein, an important substance for maintaining good health, growth, and repair. Fish cannot store protein in the body and any not used is excreted as ammonia.

ADDING FOOD
Adding organic matter, such as food, to the aquarium fuels the whole process.

In an established and well-maintained healthy aquarium, the nitrogen cycle processes waste and keep levels of ammonia, nitrites, and nitrates at a safe minimum.

NITRATES AS NUTRIENTS

Remaining nitrates are taken up by live plants as a food source. In a well-planted aquarium, the combination of water changes, denitrification, and use as a plant food source eliminate nitrate buildup. Both dead and live plant matter are consumed as an important food substance by fish, and the cycle of nitrogen compounds returns to the fish.

Even when the nitrogen cycle is working well, it is still important to carry out water changes, as other chemicals and pollutants can build up to dangerous levels. At the same time, some minerals and nutrients, vital for the physiological well-being of the fish and plants, will be used up. In an established aquarium, however, water changes can be reduced to up to a quarter of the amount recommended for new systems.

NO$_2$

NITRITE

Although not as toxic as ammonia, nitrite is still dangerous even at low levels, causing problems to fish blood and gills, and their capacity to carry oxygen. Use chemical filter media to remove excess nitrites if levels become too high.

NO$_3$

BACTERIAL CONVERSION

Working in the same fashion as Nitrosomonas spp., Nitrobacter spp. bacteria oxidize nitrites by adding an oxygen atom, creating nitrate. It is likely that a number of (unnamed) bacteria are responsible for oxidizing both ammonia and nitrite in the aquarium.

WATER CHANGES

Regular water changes dilute the concentration of nitrates in the aquarium, reducing or even preventing a harmful buildup.

DENITRIFICATION

In deeper, compacted substrates and other areas of zero oxygen (sometimes in the filter), anaerobic bacteria strip nitrate of its oxygen atoms and release nitrogen gas (N$_2$) in the process.

NITRATE

Nitrate, containing three oxygen atoms and one nitrogen atom, is far less toxic than either ammonia or nitrite. Nitrate is the end product of the biological filtration process.

The "correct" pH level of aquarium water depends on the type of fish you intend to keep. The pH level is a measure of how alkaline or acidic the water is. Some fish, such as the African Rift Lake cichlids, prefer alkaline, or high, pH conditions. Others, such as discus or dwarf cichlids, prefer acid, or low pH, conditions. The pH level is measured on a scale of 1–14, with 7 being neutral. Anything below 7 is acidic and above 7 is alkaline. Aquarium fish generally live in water with a pH level between 5 and 9. Very few fish survive happily in water with a pH level outside this range. Many fish can be acclimatized to water with a pH level different than that of their natural environment, but rarely show their best colors and may be more susceptible to disease.

The pH level is closely linked to levels of carbon dioxide in the aquarium, as carbon dioxide produces carbonic acid (acidic), which lowers pH. In planted aquariums, the pH level can fluctuate through a 24-hour period because plants produce CO_2 at night (which lowers pH) and consume it during the day by photosynthesis (which raises pH). Many fish cope easily with this change, as the same fluctuations can happen in nature.

The pH in most aquariums drops over time due to the acids produced by waste organic matter, respiration, and filtration processes. Removing waste matter and carrying out regular water changes reduce this effect. Changes in pH are damaging to fish only if they happen suddenly, for example following water changes (the pH difference between "new" and "old" water) or because of a reduction in the water's buffering capacity (see page 25).

Testing for pH

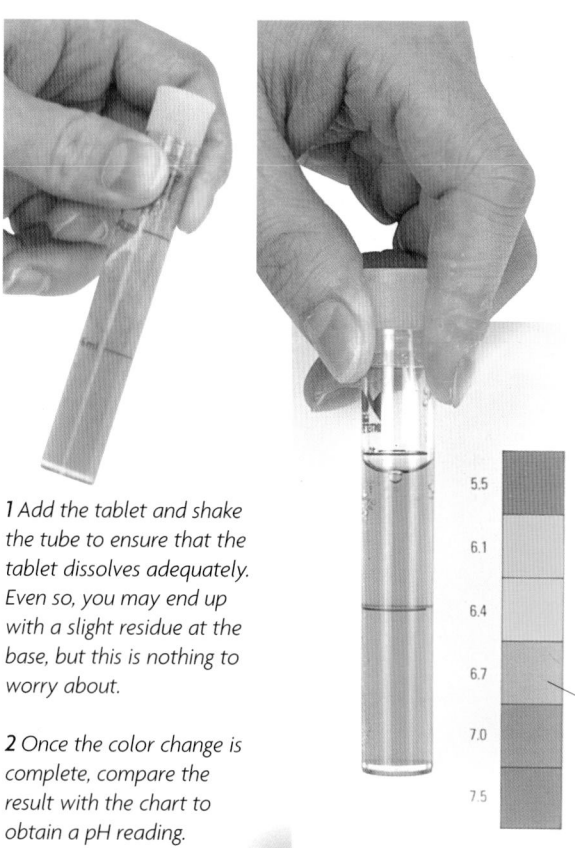

1 Add the tablet and shake the tube to ensure that the tablet dissolves adequately. Even so, you may end up with a slight residue at the base, but this is nothing to worry about.

2 Once the color change is complete, compare the result with the chart to obtain a pH reading. Hold the tube so that the color shows up well against the white card.

This test shows a pH level of about 6.7.

How is pH measured?

Water (H_2O) is made up of positively charged hydrogen ions (H^+) and negatively charged hydroxyl ions (OH^-). The pH level is a measure of the ratio of these two ions in a body of water. Acidic water has more hydrogen ions, while alkaline water contains more hydroxyl ions. Neutral water has an equal number of both.

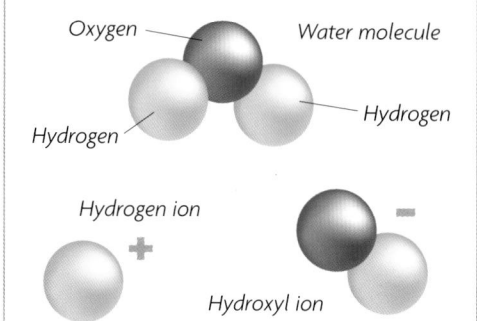

Oxygen — Water molecule

Hydrogen — Hydrogen

Hydrogen ion

Hydroxyl ion

What's in a name?

Fish that prefer acidic conditions are called acidophiles; fish that prefer alkaline conditions are called alkalophiles.

The pH scale

The pH scale is logarithmic, meaning that each unit change in pH, say from 7 to 8, is a 10 times change, a change of 2 units from 7 to 9 is a hundred times change, and from 7 to 10 reflects a thousand times change. This is why a sudden change in pH is very stressful and harmful to aquarium fish.

pH 9: 100 times more alkaline than pH 7.

pH 8: 10 times more alkaline than pH 7.

pH 7: neutral

How pH changes over a 24-hour period

During the day
Fish and plants respire, producing CO_2; plants also photosynthesize, using up CO_2. As CO_2 is being used, sufficient carbonic acid is not produced to keep pH low. Carbonates and minerals bind with acids, removing their acidic effect and raising the pH level.

At night
Plants stop photosynthesizing at night, but continue to respire, as do fish, bacteria, and other organisms. This situation creates an influx of carbon dioxide and thus, carbonic acid, which causes the pH to drop throughout the night.

Take a test at the end of the day to record the highest pH reading.

Take a test at the end of the night to record the lowest pH reading.

Water is often described as hard or soft, especially in relation to keeping certain fish species. The majority of tropical freshwater fish kept by hobbyists prefer neutral or slightly soft/acidic water. Tetras, dwarf cichlids, angelfish, and discus all enjoy softer water, while others, such as African lake cichlids, are more at home in hard water.

Water hardness is a measure of the amount of dissolved calcium and magnesium salts in the water. Water rich in calcium salts is "hard," while water with few dissolved salts is "soft." Total, or general, hardness is made up of temporary and permanent hardness and is measured in degrees of hardness (°dGH). Temporary hardness is caused by the presence of calcium bicarbonate in the water and can be removed by boiling. Permanent hardness is caused by calcium and magnesium sulphate and cannot be easily removed.

Hardness is closely linked to alkalinity because temporary hardness is mainly made up of bicarbonates, which also affect alkalinity. Hard water is usually alkaline and soft water is often acidic. Water hardness affects osmoregulation in fish (see page 48) and although fish can be acclimatized over time to abnormal water hardness levels (i.e., harder or softer than they prefer), they will be under stress and will not live as long or be as "happy."

Salinity

The salinity of water is a measure of the total dissolved salts in water and can be measured in ppt (parts per thousand), or as specific gravity. Specific gravity is a measure of the weight of water, which varies slightly with the amount of dissolved salts. The more dissolved salts contained in water, the heavier it becomes. Pure water has a specific gravity of 1 and contains no salts (0ppt), whereas seawater has a specific gravity of between 1.021 and 1.024, and contains about 35ppt salt.

Salinity is not that important for freshwater fish, but adding salts can sometimes be beneficial in a freshwater aquarium (see osmoregulation page 48). Some aquarium fish live in water that is neither seawater nor freshwater and has a salt content of up to 20ppt. These brackish water fish are found in swamps and estuaries where rivers enter the sea.

Right: A reverse osmosis unit attached to a water supply slowly forces water through a very thin molecular membrane that "sieves" out any contaminants. As salts and minerals are removed, the water has zero hardness and is so pure, that it is unsuitable for fish. Add trace elements and pH buffers to match your needs.

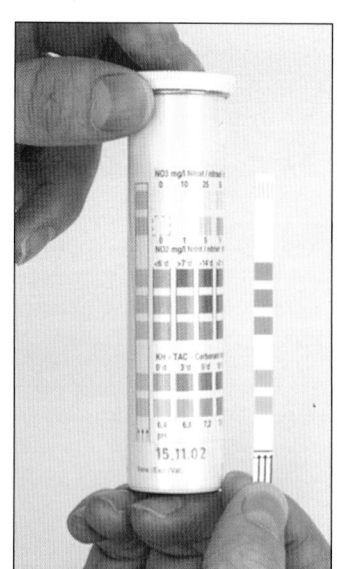

Left: This test kit uses a paper "dip strip" with chemically reactive "pads" that change color depending on the levels of certain chemicals. Dip the strip in the water for a second, leave it for 60 seconds, and then compare the color changes to the chart. This water has a low hardness and low pH, ideal for dwarf cichlids, tetras, and discus.

Levels of hardness

0–5°dGH	Very soft
6–9°dGH	Soft
10–14°dGH	Medium
15–19°dGH	Medium hard
20–28°dGH	Hard
Over 28°dGH	Very hard

Buffering capacity

Buffering capacity is the ability of a body of water to maintain a stable pH level, or more accurately, to withstand drops in pH levels. Water contains buffers, often in the form of bicarbonate and carbonate salts. These reduce fluctuations in hydrogen ions by neutralizing acids, thereby reducing any severe drops in pH. Buffering capacity is closely linked to water hardness and the same substances apply for both parameters. Hard water is generally better buffered and has a higher alkalinity (pH) than soft water. The buffering capacity of water can be kept stable by regular water changes. Over time, organic processes in the aquarium can cause a slow, continual drop in both hardness and pH. This is due to a reduction in buffering capacity as salts and minerals are used up and bind with acidic compounds. A good method of ensuring a continually high buffering capacity (in hard water aquariums only) is to use calcium-based substrates and limestone-based rock work, such as calcium gravel, ocean rock, or tufa rock.

Materials that increase hardness and pH

Ocean rock   *Calcium gravel*   *Tufa rock*

Creating soft water conditions

Reverse osmosis water 0°dGH

Dechlorinated tap water 15°dGH

pH buffer

Aquarium water 7.5°dGH / pH 6.5

Above: *A typical way of obtaining soft water is to combine reverse osmosis water with dechlorinated water and use a pH buffer to ensure stability. A 50/50 mix of R.O. water (0°dGH) and tap water (15°dGH), plus a pH buffer creates water with a pH of 6.5 and a hardness of 7.5°dGH. Vary the ratio of tap and R.O. water depending on the hardness of the tap water, and to vary the result.*

Creating hard water conditions

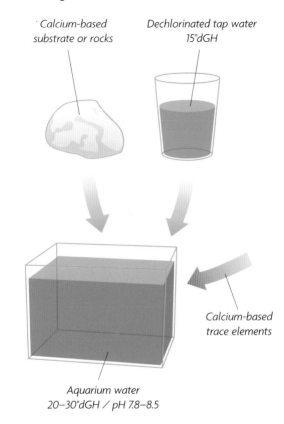

Calcium-based substrate or rocks

Dechlorinated tap water 15°dGH

Calcium-based trace elements

Aquarium water 20–30°dGH / pH 7.8–8.5

Above: *Using calcium-based substrates and rock work will help to raise hardness and maintain buffering capacity. Brand-name mixes containing salts, minerals, and trace elements can also be used in the aquarium and these will raise and maintain a high pH and hardness. Calcium-based rock work and substrates will, in most cases, prevent the pH from dropping below 7.8.*

TEMPERATURE

Water quality is not just about chemicals and pollutants. It also involves providing a stable environment for your fish, and temperature fluctuations of the water can be very damaging to life in the aquarium.

Most tropical fish can be kept at a temperature of 24–26°C (75–79°F), although some may prefer slightly warmer or cooler environments, so always check on the requirements of fish before you buy. A standard modern aquarium heater/thermostat of the right wattage should be sufficient to keep temperatures in the aquarium to within 1°C of the set level. When carrying out water changes, it is important that the new water is either within a few degrees of the aquarium water, or is introduced slowly over a period of time. In addition to the shock caused to the fish, changes in temperature can also kill filter bacteria, resulting in increased pollution levels. Keeping the temperature of the aquarium constant is mainly a matter of common sense. Avoid placing the tank near doors, radiators, and direct sunlight, as well as any areas where the ambient temperature is too high or very low.

Sometimes a change in temperature can be a good thing for your fish; in certain species it can trigger spawning, and a rapid increase by a couple of degrees can kill some diseases, but only try this if you know exactly what you are doing.

Low oxygen in warm water

Oxygen levels are reduced at higher temperatures. During the summer it can be hard to control temperature, so the fish may appreciate extra aeration.

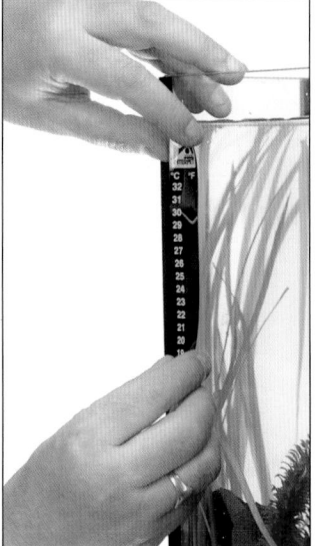

Often called a digital thermometer, this type can be attached to the outside of the aquarium.

This thermometer goes inside the aquarium and provides a more accurate reading than the stick-on types.

Right: Before installing a heater/thermostat, adjust the temperature setting to suit your fish. Most heater/thermostats can be set to maintain a temperature in the range of 18–32°C (64–90°F).

Below: Installing a digital thermometer is easy. Simply remove the covering strip to expose the adhesive back and stick it directly onto the glass.

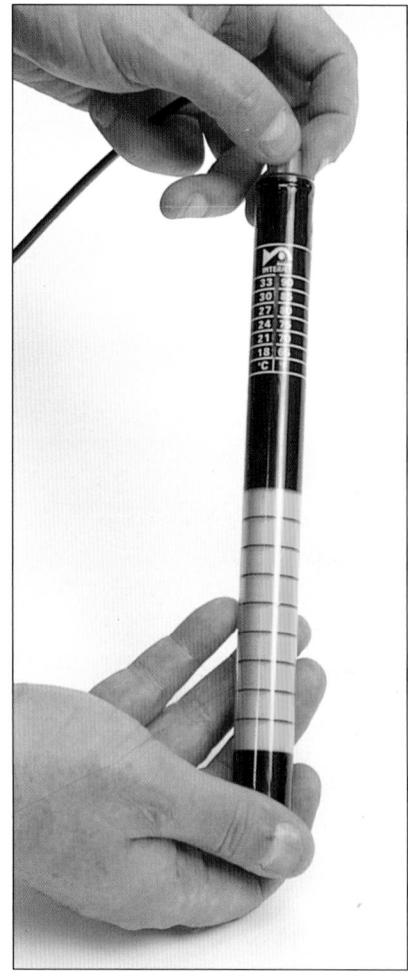

How temperature affects ammonia toxicity

% free (toxic) ammonia
in total ammonia

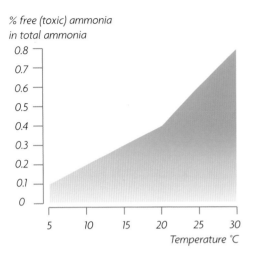

Temperature °C

Ammonia is found in two forms: free ammonia and ammonium. Free ammonia is the most toxic form, but only makes up a small percentage of the total ammonia. Both temperature and pH affect the ratio of free ammonia and ammonium. At higher temperatures and pH levels, more free ammonia can be found. This graph shows the temperature effect at pH 7 (neutral). At pH 8, the percentage of free ammonia increases tenfold.

How temperature affects oxygen levels

Oxygen mg/liter

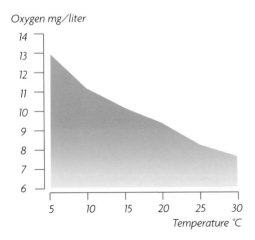

Temperature °C

As the temperature of water rises, the amount of oxygen that can be dissolved in it before saturation is reached falls. As temperature rises, fish need more oxygen to survive. A rise in temperature also causes an increase in the rate of plant and animal metabolism. This, in turn, means that fish, plants, and bacteria use up more oxygen at higher temperatures, thereby increasing the risk of oxygen deficiency.

Above: *Neon tetras (Paracheirodon innesi) are among the most popular aquarium fish. They are sensitive to changes in water quality, and it is vital to allow them to adjust slowly to the temperature of their new home when adding them to the aquarium.*

Testing for oxygen level

Test kits are available to monitor oxygen levels, but they are not an essential item of equipment. If you think there may be a problem with a lack of oxygen in your aquarium, it is important to test at the right time. Oxygen levels fluctuate throughout the day, so readings taken at the wrong time may be inaccurate. The best time to take a reading is at the end of the night before light starts to enter the aquarium. This is when oxygen levels are likely to be at their lowest and plants have not begun to photosynthesize.

The filter is by far the most important piece of equipment in the aquarium. Without some form of filtration your fish will not live. The aquarium is a "closed environment" and in effect, your fish live in their own toilet; filtration simply provides the flush. Filters are available in many forms and perform three main functions: the removal of visible waste and debris; the circulation and aeration of water, and the removal of toxic organic pollutants. First, here are the main processes of filtration.

Mechanical filtration

The removal of any visible particles in the water is more important to the fishkeeper than to the fish. The fish do not especially mind if the water looks slightly dirty; in fact, this probably resembles their natural habitat more closely. However, fishkeepers prefer crystal clear water, and good mechanical filtration achieves this. Mechanical filtration involves straining the water through a medium, such as foam, to trap any particles. Mechanical media are supplied in various grades (coarse, medium, fine) to trap different sized particles. Filter floss is often used as a final "polishing"

Right: In the natural environment, filtration is carried out by bacteria in the substrate and through plants, both aquatic and terrestrial. The large volume of water compared to animal mass allows wastes to be quickly diluted and removed.

Green water
Green water is caused by single-celled algae (see page 53), which may not be removed by mechanical filtration.

Types of filter media

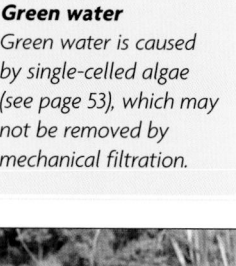

As a final "polishing" medium, filter floss removes anything visible left in the water. Once the floss is clogged up or dirty, it should be replaced, rather than cleaned.

Large-grade sponge removes the larger visible particles in the aquarium. These are then broken down by bacteria into smaller particles.

medium to remove the smallest particles from the water. Regular removal of wastes by methods such as gravel cleaning (see page 39) can also be regarded as mechanical filtration.

Biological filtration

The most important filtration process is biological filtration, which is the breakdown and removal of organic pollutants, such as ammonia and nitrites, by bacteria. Most toxic organic pollutants cannot be visibly detected in the water, so without adequate biological filtration, your water could be crystal clear, yet deadly. A biological filter medium is one with a high surface area on which bacteria can settle and remove pollutants by a process of oxidation. This process is explained as part of the nitrogen cycle (see pages 20–21). The media used for mechanical filtration, such as foams, often double as biological media. For larger filters and external filters, you can use specially designed biological media, such as sintered glass or ceramic nodules, which have a much increased surface area, that provide more efficient and balanced biological filtration.

These sintered glass pieces provide an enormous surface area for beneficial bacteria to colonize.

These ceramic nodules (in white and dark gray), are another biological medium. They have a large surface area and their shape allows water to pass through easily, which prevents the filter from clogging.

These hollow ceramic cylinders make an excellent mechanical filter medium that traps dirt particles and yet allows an even flow of water through the filter.

These solid cylinders are also sintered glass with a rough, pitted surface, ideal for oxygen-loving bacteria to colonize.

Cloudy water

If your water turns cloudy or a milky color you may be experiencing a bacterial bloom. This can happen during the first week of an aquarium's life or if the filtration process breaks down. Test the water for any pollutants and add a bacterial starter. This contains live bacteria that will help the filter to process waste and achieve a suitably sized colony of bacteria in the filter medium.

What to do during a power outage

The bacteria that carry out biological filtration depend on a constant flow of water through the filter (mainly to provide oxygen), as well as a reasonably stable temperature. During power outages and maintenance, the bacteria will not receive this flow and may start to die off after a few hours. Not only will this stop biological filtration from taking place, but the dying bacteria may also release pollutants into the water. If, for any reason, the filter is switched off for more than two or three hours, clean the media in aquarium water, which can then be thrown away, and treat the tank with a bacterial starter. It would also be wise to stop feeding for a few days, or feed only minimal amounts, and increase the frequency of small water changes to reduce the buildup of waste matter.

29

CHEMICAL FILTRATION

In addition to organic pollutants, other pollutants, such as metals and unwanted chemicals, can also enter the aquarium. To remove these and to assist in the removal of organic pollutants, you can use chemical filtration. Basically, chemical filtration is any form of filtration that alters the water's properties, and includes water softeners and even dechlorinators. Some chemical media, such as activated carbon, have a limited life span. If they are left in the aquarium too long, they will reach a point where they cannot contain any more pollutants, and may even release pollutants back into the tank. Apart from activated carbon, which is included in many filters, most chemical media need only be used when necessary, and are not a vital part of the filtration process.

Activated carbon removes phosphates, nitrates, and airborne pollutants, among others. Activated carbon also removes discoloration, often caused by bogwood.

Some chemical media, such as zeolite, can be "recharged" and used again by soaking them overnight in a concentrated salt solution.

Using medications

When treating the tank with any medications, remove chemical media such as carbon, otherwise they will absorb the medication and render it useless.

Ultraviolet light sterilization

This is rarely used in home aquariums, but is worth mentioning. Passing water through an ultraviolet sterilizer (UVS), a unit containing an ultraviolet (UV) tube, will destroy single-celled algae and bacteria. Sterilization reduces disease in the aquarium by killing any disease pathogens in the water as they pass through the UV light. However, passing water through a sterilizer may also render many treatments useless. Ultraviolet clarifiers (UVCs) are used as part of the filtration process in ponds to destroy algae. The only difference between a clarifier (UVC) and a sterilizer (UVS) is that the clarifier has a greater distance between the light tube and the outer reaches of the water inside the unit. This distance reduces the light's power and its ability to kill disease pathogens, but it will still kill algae. It also allows more water to pass through the unit.

Specific problems

Chemical media are available for specific purposes, such as the removal of ammonia, nitrites, nitrates, and metals. Use them as short-term solutions to water quality problems.

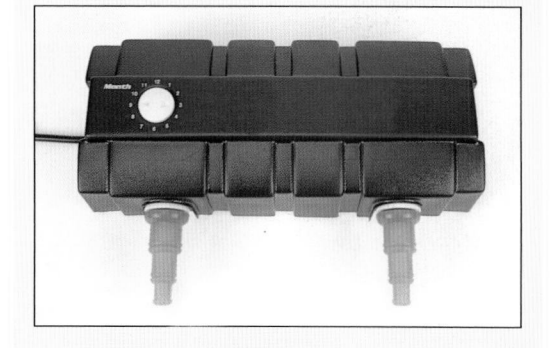

UNDERGRAVEL FILTRATION

Many types of aquarium filters are available, although they usually fall into one of three categories: undergravel, internal, and external. Choosing the right filter depends on the kind of fish you are going to keep and the type of aquarium you are setting up.

Undergravel filtration was once the most popular method of aquarium filtration, but now there are many better alternatives. However, it may be suitable for some aquariums, such as small ones, where space needs to be optimized, aquariums with young fry (fry may be sucked into a conventional filter), or with fish that do not appreciate strong water flows. The filter works by drawing aquarium water through the gravel substrate and returning it at the water surface. The substrate acts as a biological and mechanical medium, trapping particles and providing a suitably sized area for bacteria to grow on and remove organic pollutants. The filter consists of an undergravel plate placed on the aquarium floor, plus one or more uplift tubes, and can be powered either by an air pump or a powerhead (water pump).

Undergravel filters take up very little space in the aquarium and the visible uplift tubes and/or pumps are easy to hide. However, the chief disadvantage of undergravel filters is the impossibility of removing the biologically active medium (the gravel) from the aquarium in order to protect the flora of nitrifiers from the many medications that are toxic to these bacteria. This means that the fishkeeper has less control over the filtration process. The aquarist confronted with a disease outbreak thus is faced with a no-win situation – treat the fish and kill the tank's filter, or do nothing and lose the fish.

Above: Using a powerhead instead of an air pump creates a stronger, more constant flow rate, thus increasing the efficiency of the undergravel filter. Powerheads can be raised or lowered to adjust oxygenation.

Above: The undergravel filter plate has a series of small slits placed between rows of raised "channels" through which water is drawn. These provide an even flow across the whole substrate. Depending on the size of aquarium, you may have one, two, or even three uplift tubes.

Add enough substrate

Make sure there is a sufficient depth of substrate for the bacteria to colonize. About 5 cm (2 in) should be sufficient.

Choose the right gravel

Use only natural gravel in an undergravel filter. Colored gravels often have smooth surfaces that make them less efficient at biological filtration. For the same reason, try to avoid large-grade substrates.

INTERNAL & EXTERNAL FILTERS

The internal power filter is the most common and effective method of filtration in smaller aquariums. Most internal power filters are a simple combination of a suitably sized sponge medium and a pump to circulate water. The sponge provides mechanical filtration (by trapping particles that can then be removed) and biological filtration (by providing a surface area for bacteria to colonize). The whole unit is relatively small and can be placed in a back corner of the aquarium near the water surface to provide surface agitation. Some internal power filters contain additional biological and chemical media in separate compartments, increasing the filter's effectiveness. Many are supplied with a venturi. By attaching an airline to the outflow of the filter/pump, air is drawn into the flow, increasing surface movement and oxygenation. In terms of cost, internal power filters are similar in price to all the equipment needed for an undergravel filter and are a much better option.

Internal air-powered filters

Working on the same principle as the internal power filter, water is drawn through a sponge that provides mechanical and biological filtration. However, instead of being powered by a water pump, the system incorporates a much less powerful air pump, ideal for small tanks and for fish that do not like water movement. The filter is not as effective as a power filter and should only be used in aquariums with low stocking levels or heavy planting. Air-powered filters are also ideal for tanks with young fry, as the minimal flow and open design eliminate the problem of fry being sucked into the filter.

Replacing lost bacteria

When cleaning the filter sponge (in dechlorinated or aquarium water) some bacteria will inevitably be lost. To help reduce this loss, cut the filter sponge in half and clean each half alternately. The uncleaned sponge helps replenish bacteria into the cleaned sponge. Use the same method when replacing the sponge.

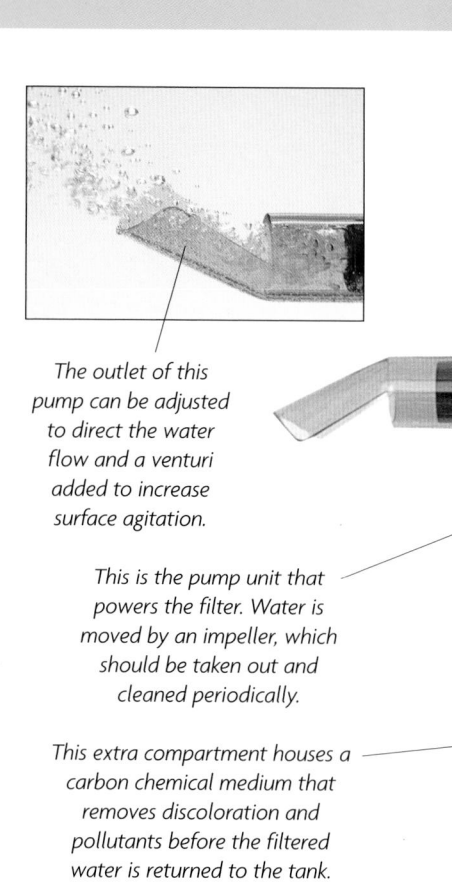

The outlet of this pump can be adjusted to direct the water flow and a venturi added to increase surface agitation.

This is the pump unit that powers the filter. Water is moved by an impeller, which should be taken out and cleaned periodically.

This extra compartment houses a carbon chemical medium that removes discoloration and pollutants before the filtered water is returned to the tank.

Inside the casing is the sponge through which water is drawn, trapping particles and housing beneficial bacteria.

Above: *This small air-powered filter contains biological, chemical, and mechanical media, ideal for small aquariums or for young fry.*

External power filters

External power filters are by far the most effective, giving the fishkeeper complete control over the filtration process. Water is drawn out of the tank to the filter, passed through various filtration media, and is returned to the tank via a spray bar, venturi, or outlet tube. External filters incorporate compartments that allow you to separate mechanical, biological, and chemical media. Their increased mechanical capacity makes them an ideal choice for aquariums housing large, messy fish.

Another popular type of external filter is a rotary impeller-driven unit designed to hang on the back of the aquarium.

Small tanks and goldfish bowls

It is worth mentioning here the subject of small tanks without filters, including goldfish bowls. A well-meaning but ignorant fishkeeper may recall their own or someone else's fish that "lived quite happily for years" in a bowl without filtration. First, these fish are not happy and probably would have lived for many more years and grown much larger if they had been kept in the correct conditions. Second, even hardy fish, such as goldfish, will not "live happily" in poor conditions; they merely tolerate them for long periods of time before they finally die from incorrect care. Keeping fish in bowls, or unfiltered, small aquariums, must be considered cruel and pointless. After all, you would never think of keeping a cat or dog in a small cage with unclean surroundings.

Types of filter media

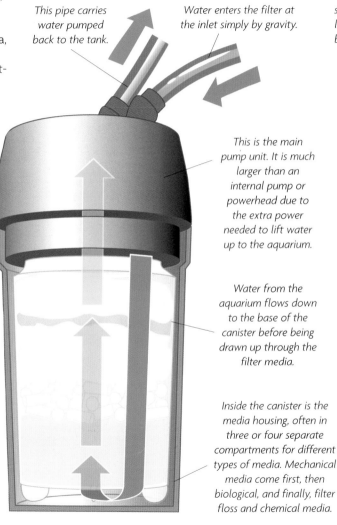

This pipe carries water pumped back to the tank.

Water enters the filter at the inlet simply by gravity.

This is the main pump unit. It is much larger than an internal pump or powerhead due to the extra power needed to lift water up to the aquarium.

Water from the aquarium flows down to the base of the canister before being drawn up through the filter media.

Inside the canister is the media housing, often in three or four separate compartments for different types of media. Mechanical media come first, then biological, and finally, filter floss and chemical media.

The inlet pipe has a strainer on the end to stop large objects and fish from being sucked into the filter.

You can place the return at the water surface, or lower if you wish, to reduce oxygen levels in a planted aquarium.

The filter sits underneath the aquarium. When you clean the filter, place it inside a bucket or bowl to reduce spillage.

Maintaining good water quality and a healthy environment for your fish requires a biologically and chemically balanced system. It may take several weeks or even months for your aquarium to mature to the point where it becomes a stable environment. During this maturation period, take care that the system does not "overload" and that water quality remains as near to ideal as possible. The main biological process that you are trying to establish in the aquarium is the nitrogen cycle.

Helping the nitrogen cycle

In an ideal world, the nitrogen cycle would take care of itself in the aquarium and keep water quality in check without the fishkeeper having to worry. Unfortunately, things are never that simple and it is vital that the fishkeeper keeps things running smoothly, including giving the nitrogen cycle a helping hand. Making sure that the nitrogen cycle works effectively depends on regular maintenance and ensuring that the system is not overloaded. The aquarium and the filtration system can only cope with a certain amount of waste, and there are a few methods to ensure that it is kept to a minimum.

Controlled feeding is essential (see page 42). However, during the first few weeks or months of an aquarium, it may be worth avoiding high protein foods until the nitrogen cycle is well established and able to cope with the increased volume of waste.

Removing nitrites and nitrates

As discussed on page 30, chemical media can help to remove toxins, reducing the load on bacteria and the nitrogen cycle. Ideally, biological filtration should be able to cope alone, but in new aquariums, or in cases of increased load, use chemical filtration to help the nitrogen cycle become established with minimal problems.

Introducing bacteria

The addition of live bacteria helps the nitrogen cycle establish quickly and increases the efficiency of waste breakdown and/or removal. There are a number of ways to introduce bacteria (Nitrosomonas and Nitrobacter spp.) into the aquarium and filtration system. These bacteria are always present in small numbers, but until the fish are introduced there is not sufficient volume to cope with any significant amount of waste. The most common method of introducing bacteria is through the use of a biological/bacterial starter, readily available off the shelf from aquatic retailers. Bacterial starters have a wide range of effectiveness. Nevertheless, there are two forms – pure live bacteria, and live bacteria with a food source – and they are usually in liquid or powder form. Live bacteria are concentrated numbers of bacteria directly introduced to the aquarium. Most of these will probably die off, but those that settle will form the basis of biological filtration. Live bacteria with a food source is a mixture of bacteria and an ammonia substance. The ammonia provides the bacteria with a source of food, allowing the bacteria that settle to begin processing waste immediately, thus accelerating the maturation process. There are advantages and disadvantages to both methods. Introducing bacteria with a food source – and consequently introducing toxic ammonia to the aquarium – obviously can be dangerous, but if a balance can be achieved (meaning the bacteria are using up all the ammonia) before any fish are introduced, then the stress on the fish is

Biological/bacterial starters

This liquid starter contains bacterial cultures to "kick-start" biological filters. Simply add the required amount to a jug of aquarium water, stir, and pour over the surface.

These slow-release capsules contain enzymes to aid waste breakdown and compounds to encourage bacteria. Add as directed to the filter or aquarium.

Above: *Using a bacterial starter correctly reduces the water quality problems that can occur in a new aquarium.*

much reduced. Live bacteria without a food source may not colonize in sufficient numbers to cope with all the waste introduced with new fish. However, no toxic ammonia is added and the bacteria can be added continually while fish are in the aquarium. Whichever method you choose, live bacteria should be added continually throughout the first two months of the aquarium's life to aid maturation. Do this daily with pure bacteria starters, or weekly if you are using the bacteria plus food type of starter.

Maturing the aquarium

When the aquarium is first set up it is biologically inactive, which means that none of the usual biological processes, many of which make up the nitrogen cycle, are taking place. To become a healthy environment for fish, the aquarium needs to mature, a process that will take, on average, about six weeks. During this time it is important to take great care with stocking, feeding, and maintenance, as well as observing a few other guidelines to help maturation.

Once the aquarium is filled with water and the substrate has been washed and put in place, turn on and check all the aquarium equipment. Make sure that the filter is pumping constantly and at a steady flow, and that once the correct temperature is reached, there are no fluctuations. Check the temperature at various times (morning, mid-afternoon and

Day and night

If you introduce plants early on before the fish, make sure that any lighting is timed to go on and off as normal. Plants need regular periods of light and darkness, and as lighting affects plant photosynthesis (see page 14), it also affects the water quality.

night) to ensure that it remains constant throughout the day. Even though you are not introducing any fish yet, it is worth using a dechlorinator to remove any chloramines that may be present in the water (see page 16). After 24 hours, or when the temperature has stabilized, you can add the plants. Now that you have the beginnings of the aquarium, you can look at adding some biological activity and getting the nitrogen cycle started.

Maturing the aquarium

Once the aquarium water is heated and dechlorinated, you can add the plants. Live plants help to remove some of the waste matter produced by the fish.

Introducing the first fish

The longer the aquarium is left without fish the better, but sometimes this is not practical, and in any case, you will be eager to stock the tank. Even so, aim to leave the tank empty for at least seven days. After this time you can be sure that all the equipment is working properly and that the aquarium water has matured a little. At this stage, even with the addition of a bacterial starter, the filter

Leave the filter running continuously and add a biological starter. This ensures that the filtration system is better equipped to cope with waste matter when the fish are introduced.

Use an aquarium thermometer to check that the water temperature is correct and remains stable.

Although there are no fish in the aquarium, it is always worth testing the water for ammonia, nitrites, and nitrates, that may already be present.

is not ready to cope with the influx of waste from feeding and fish. Because of this, only introduce a few of the hardiest fish. Leave a gap of at least one week between the introduction of each batch of fish. When the fish are introduced, the biological load on the aquarium is suddenly increased, and it will take a while for the system and the filter to get rid of any increase in pollutants and then reach a level where they can cope with the increased waste.

Water testing

Testing the water is extremely important during the maturation process. Without testing the water, you will not be able to tell how well the system is doing, and if things don't go well you may lose some, or all, of your fish. Testing the water greatly reduces the chances of this happening. There are a few things to look for when testing the water to make sure that maturation and the nitrogen cycle are working as effectively as possible. Before you introduce any fish, levels of ammonia and nitrites should be zero. You may get a reading of nitrates, as some domestic water supplies do contain them, but providing the levels are not high,

Keep track

Keep a chart of test results for your own aquarium so that you can see how well it is maturing. Mark any introductions of fish, or changes in feeding, or maintenance regimes so you can see how they affect the aquarium.

New tank syndrome

When you begin fishkeeping, you will no doubt hear of something called "new tank syndrome." This occurs when water quality fluctuations (mainly ammonia and nitrites) adversely affect fish. Even with the best care, you may lose one or two fish to new tank syndrome, so prepare to expect this. If the aquarium is stocked too quickly, incorrectly maintained, or the fish are overfed, new tank syndrome can have drastic effects and may even kill all the fish within a short period of time. Many good retailers have their own information leaflets on new tank syndrome and on maturing your aquarium, so do not be afraid to ask.

this should not cause a problem. As you introduce bacterial starters, you may get a small ammonia or nitrite reading. This is normal and should dissipate within a few days. Check the water before adding any fish and again 24 hours later. You should expect a slight ammonia reading, but this should drop within the next 24 hours. If not, there may be a problem with the bacteria establishing.

Each time you introduce more fish you may get a slight increase in ammonia, followed by a slight nitrite increase. This is perfectly normal, and providing optimum conditions are restored within 48 hours, you have nothing much to worry about. As time goes on, this effect will be reduced, because the filter will contain more bacteria and be able to adapt more quickly. The chart below shows what may happen during a maturation period of six weeks.

Above: *When introducing fish, float the bag in the tank with the lights switched off for about 20 minutes to equalize temperatures. Although it takes fish a number of days to adjust to the change in water conditions, you may wish to add small quantities of aquarium water to the bag every five minutes to ease their introduction to the tank.*

How the biological filter matures during the first few weeks of a new aquarium

Ammonia mg/l — Nitrite mg/l — Nitrate mg/l

Week 1
There are no fish in the aquarium. The ammonia and nitrite peaks are caused by the addition of a biological starter. Bacteria become established and turn ammonia into nitrites and nitrites into nitrates.

Week 2
Fish are introduced, causing waste that turns into ammonia. The bacteria already present start to convert this into nitrite and nitrate. More bacteria will colonize the filter media to cope with the increase in waste/ammonia.

Week 3
Now a few more fish can be added. The already established filter bacteria can cope much better with the excess ammonia this causes. Note the growing level of nitrate, which is reduced at the end of each week by a 25 percent water change.

Week 4
Introducing more fish now has a much reduced effect. During the first six-week period, a biological starter is added every week, ensuring that bacteria quickly colonize the filter when fish are added.

Week 5
Adding fish has hardly any effect on the levels of ammonia and nitrite. This is because the bacteria in the filter have reached a population that can quickly adapt to any changes.

Week 6
The filter is fully established and the aquarium is starting to mature. More sensitive fish can now be added. Check nitrate levels; you may need to make partial water changes or use a chemical filter media to reduce them.

Week 1 | Week 2 | Week 3 | Week 4 | Week 5 | Week 6

No matter how good your filtration system, there is always a need for regular maintenance in the aquarium. The regular removal of organic wastes, water changes, and general tidying up will keep the aquarium looking its best and the fish as healthy as possible. Maintaining a tropical freshwater aquarium is not a major undertaking and, if done regularly, only takes about 30 minutes a week (depending on the size of the aquarium). It is distressing to hear stories of fishkeepers who regularly remove all their fish to a separate container and completely clean the aquarium, gravel, and decor before replacing the water and fish. This form of maintenance is incredibly damaging to the aquarium environment and to the fish.

Water changes

Even if everything seems fine in the aquarium and the water is crystal clear, regular water changes are still essential. Over time, trace elements that are important to both fish and plants diminish, and organic pollutants, such as nitrates, build up and may not be removed by filtration. Regular, small water changes will dilute any pollutants and replace lost trace elements.

Any sudden change of environment can be stressful to fish, so keep the amount of water changed to a minimum. The quantity of water and the frequency of water changes are subjects on which you will hear many different opinions, even from expert fishkeepers. It is true that some aquariums can be left for far longer periods of time without any need for water changes, but to judge

this accurately, you would need the backing of many years of fishkeeping experience. To be safe, make a weekly water change of 15–20 percent in an unplanted aquarium and a 20–25 percent change every two weeks in a heavily planted aquarium. The reason for the difference is that plants can remove many of the nitrates in the aquarium, thus reducing the need for water changes. The smaller the water change, the less stress is placed on the aquarium environment, so ideally, carry out small water changes every few days.

Introducing the water

Water changes can be stressful and damaging to fish if they are not carried out correctly. The new water should be similar, if not identical, to that in the tank in terms of hardness, pH, and temperature to avoid any shock. Providing the water in the aquarium is unaltered in terms of water quality, and the source of the new water is the same, there should be no problems. To raise the temperature of the new water, let it stand for 24 hours and heat it with a small aquarium heater/thermostat. Mixing boiled water with cooler water to raise the temperature before introducing it to the aquarium is possible, but may reduce hardness. If heating the water is not

Switch off

When making water changes, ensure that the water level does not drop below the heater/ thermostat, internal filter, or external filter inlet. If this cannot be avoided, turn off any relevant equipment.

Water changers and substrate cleaners

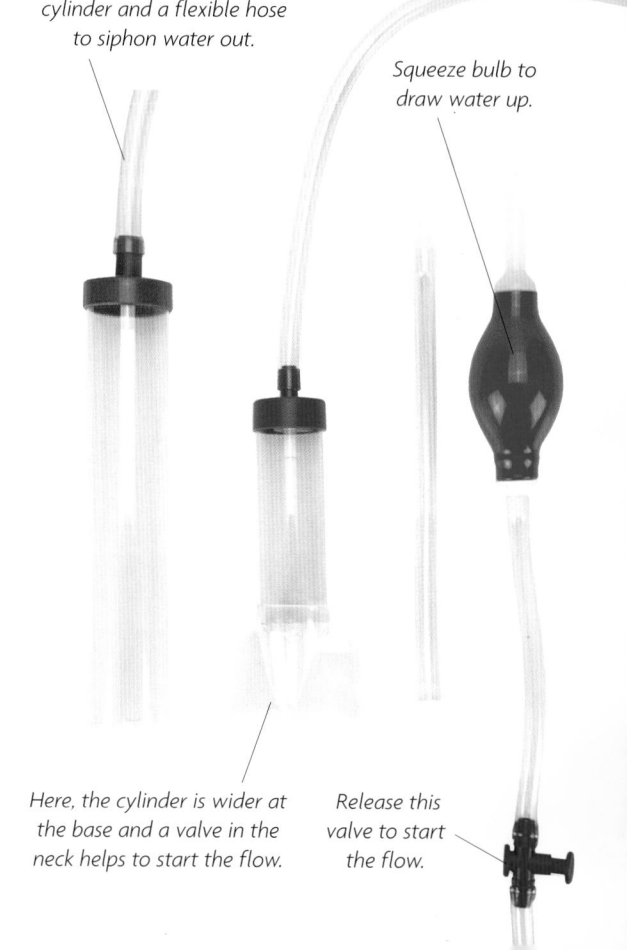

This design has a simple rigid cylinder and a flexible hose to siphon water out.

Squeeze bulb to draw water up.

Here, the cylinder is wider at the base and a valve in the neck helps to start the flow.

Release this valve to start the flow.

Above: You may be surprised at the large amount of waste matter that collects in the substrate. This gravel cleaner removes waste debris from the substrate, helping to maintain good water quality.

possible, leave it in a heated room for 24 hours and introduce it to the aquarium slowly over a period of an hour or more. Providing you add the water slowly and carefully over time, most fish are not bothered by a small drop in temperature.

If you are using tap water, be sure to dechlorinate it first. There are two methods of doing this. Using a brand-name dechlorinator, some of which also remove chloramines, is by far the best method. These are supplied in a liquid form and you simply add the correct dosage to the water (see page 16). They dechlorinate the water within a few minutes; sometimes you can even smell the difference. The second method is to aerate the water for 24 hours. This increases the gas exchange and allows chlorine to dissipate into the atmosphere.

Finally, when introducing the new water, pour it slowly to avoid disturbing the substrate or decor, and make sure that any containers are reserved solely for the aquarium and never used for any other purpose. Chemical residues can remain in containers for long periods of time and be harmful to aquatic life.

Cleaning the substrate

Although filtration removes some visible particles from the water, its main function is biological – to remove organic pollutants. Most of the physical waste in the aquarium ends up trapped in the substrate and must be removed to reduce the buildup of bacteria and remove organic pollutants released by the breakdown of waste. Too much waste in the gravel increases bacteria levels and can cause disease in some fish; bottom-feeders, such as *Corydoras*, are particularly susceptible. The easy way to remove waste from the substrate is with one of the many gravel cleaners on the market. Place this simple siphon device in the substrate and it lifts away the

waste matter while agitating the substrate, and then deposits the substrate back on the aquarium floor. Agitating the substrate and removing waste also help to prevent algae buildup. Siphon the water that is removed, along with all waste matter, to waste. Because the process removes water from the aquarium, do a gravel cleaning at the same time as a water change. You can then replace the lost water with the new water you have prepared for the aquarium.

Most gravel cleaners are supplied with various self-start mechanisms, making the whole process very simple to carry out. Battery-powered and air-powered gravel cleaners are also available. These recycle the water back to the aquarium and remove waste via a strainer, but they are often not as effective, or as powerful, as a siphon-based cleaner. Clean the aquarium gravel at least twice a month.

Gravel cleaners may not be effective on finer substrates, such as sand, as they are likely to remove the sand as well as the waste. To clean this kind of substrate, simply siphon the waste from the surface, where it settles, and then stir the substrate thoroughly to prevent stagnation.

Filter maintenance

Your filter needs regular maintenance to keep it working efficiently and to prolong its useful life. Properly maintained, a good filter will last for many years. The three most common forms of filtration in a freshwater aquarium are undergravel, internal power filter, and external power filter. Each system requires a different maintenance regime.

Undergravel filters need virtually no maintenance and will continue to work effectively with regular gravel cleaning. Replace the airstone every six months. Every few years, you will notice a reduction in power or air flow, which means the air pump diaphragm has worn out and needs replacing. If you are using powerheads with your undergravel filter, clean the impellers every few months according to the manufacturer's directions. An impeller is the device in virtually all power filters and pumps that moves the water. It consists of three main parts: a magnet, a series of blades or fins, and the impeller shaft. The magnet and blades are connected and should slide easily out of the pump. Simply wipe them clean. The impeller housing (where the impeller was) can be cleaned with a small brush or old toothbrush. Some impeller shafts are fixed, while others can be removed. They are usually ceramic or metal. When cleaning the pump, be careful not to break or bend the impeller shaft.

Internal filter sponges should be removed and cleaned in water from the aquarium, not in tap water. The chlorine contained in tap water will kill the beneficial bacteria on which the whole filtration process is based. Do not clean the sponge too

Left: A well-maintained filter keeps the aquarium water clean and clear, allowing your fish and plants to thrive.

Maintenance chart

✓ New aquarium / first four weeks   ✓ Established aquarium

This is a typical maintenance regime for a standard tropical aquarium. Use it as a guideline to preparing a maintenance chart for your own aquarium.

	DAILY	TWICE WEEKLY	WEEKLY	EVERY 2 WEEKS	MONTHLY	EVERY 3 MONTHS	YEARLY	AS NEEDED
Check for dead fish, signs of disease, bullying, abnormal behavior.	✓✓							
Check equipment, temperature, flow rate, etc.	✓✓							
Remove dead plant matter.			✓✓					

Left: *Use a bowl or bucket in which to clean filter material. Use a new container the first time you clean the filter and then keep it solely for aquarium use.*

thoroughly, as bacteria can be removed along with other waste. The frequency of cleaning depends on the individual aquarium, but most internal filters need cleaning once a month. If the flow rate of the pump/filter starts to decrease, it may need cleaning more often. The impeller also needs maintaining.

External filters are not as easy to maintain, but usually need cleaning less often than internal filters. Once again, the sponges should only be cleaned in aquarium water, which can then be thrown away. Any other biological media in the filter can also be rinsed in aquarium water, but unless they are visibly dirty, they only need be cleaned once every three months or so. Replace filter floss every time the filter is maintained. The floss is simply a final "polishing" medium to remove small particles and has virtually no influence on biological filtration. Open and prime the filter according to the manufacturer's instructions; it may be worth placing the filter in a container to avoid any spillages.

Task						
Clean the substrate			✓	✓		
Water change 10–20 percent Sparsely planted or heavily stocked with fish	✓	✓				
Water change 10–20 percent Heavily planted or sparsely stocked with fish			✓	✓		
Clean filter sponge in aquarium water or dechlorinated water			✓	✓		
Replace carbon media in filter					✓ ✓	
Clean pump impeller					✓ ✓	
Replace light tube (only vital in planted tanks)						✓
Partially replace biological filter media						✓ ✓
Clean aquarium glass and remove algae						✓ ✓
Trim plants						✓ ✓

To maintain good water quality and healthy fish, it is important to regulate and control the amount of waste entering the aquarium. Virtually all the waste in the aquarium originates from feeding.

Flake food

The type of food you use affects the overall health and color of your fish. Dried flake food is the most commonly used food and also one of the best. It consists of a dried mix of food, with added vitamins, minerals, and roughage that provide the fish with all their basic needs. Virtually all common fish accept flake food; indeed, some enjoy it so much that it may cause problems. When it enters the aquarium, dried food quickly expands and absorbs water as it floats on the surface. If the fish eat too much of it before it has had a chance to expand, it may expand and release air inside the fish, causing temporary buoyancy problems. Most fish cope with this by simply releasing the gas, but some species, especially fancy goldfish, may experience longer term

Flake food forms the main diet for most tropical fish, and should be offered in small quantities. Take care not to overfeed, as uneaten food can soon pollute the aquarium water.

problems. To avoid this, simply prevent the fish from reaching the food for a few moments or place the food in a separate small container of water for a few seconds before putting it in the aquarium.

Pellet foods and wafers

For larger fish, such as some cichlids, you can buy pellet foods, both sinking and floating. If your fish take food from the surface, always use the floating pellets. They give you more control over feeding, as any leftovers are easy to remove. Sinking pellets can be used for catfish that feed from the aquarium floor. Sinking "wafers" are also available. These are much larger and do not break down quickly, so are ideal for feeding large catfish or a group of smaller catfish, such as *Corydoras* sp. Offer wafers every other day. Place them in the aquarium for up to an hour before removing any leftovers.

Algae wafers made from vegetable matter are ideal for herbivorous algae-eaters and bottom-feeding catfish.

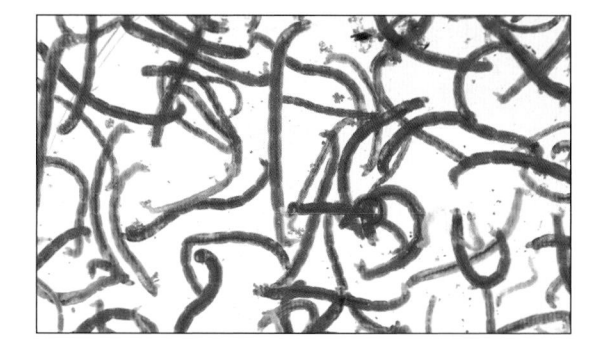

Above: Frozen or live foods, such as these bloodworms, can be fed as a treat and as an important supplement to the main diet.

Live and frozen foods

Live foods are readily available and a good source of protein, as well as a "treat" for fish. Generally, they are very safe, providing they are obtained from a reliable retailer. The most common live foods include bloodworm, daphnia, brine shrimp, and tubifex. Most fish can be offered live or frozen foods two or three times a week as an alternative to the basic diet of flake or dried food. Live foods should be strained through a fine net to remove the water they are supplied in and you may also prefer to rinse them briefly before putting them in the aquarium.

The frozen foods available today lose very little nutritional value during the freezing process and some contain additional vitamins and minerals.

Simply break off a suitably sized chunk and hold it just below the water surface. The block will soon melt and come apart and the fish may even take the food straight from your fingers. Frozen shrimp and fish are also available for larger fish.

Storing food

Apart from frozen foods (which should be kept frozen) and live foods (which should be fed as soon as possible), store all food sealed and away from direct sunlight in a dry place. Over time, foods lose their vitamin and nutrient content. Most have a use-by date and should always be consumed within a few months of opening. Depending on the freshness of live food when you buy it, you can keep it in a refrigerator or cool area for a few days without too much loss of quality.

Feeding quantity

There is no set quantity or formula relating to how much or even how often you should feed your fish. It is simply a case of trial and error, but there are a few useful guidelines. Most fish deaths experienced by new fishkeepers occur as a result of bad water

Feeding in a new aquarium

Some foods, such as frozen and live foods, are very high in protein, which breaks down into ammonia in the aquarium. For this reason, it is wise not to use high protein foods in a new aquarium for a few weeks until the filter is sufficiently established to cope with the larger amounts of waste. Fish need protein for growth and repair and also to maintain their immune system. High protein foods are ideal for fish that are ill, stressed, or preparing to breed.

quality, and more often than not, bad water quality is caused by overfeeding. Overfeeding and uneaten food increases the levels of toxic ammonia, nitrites and, eventually, nitrates. They also promote adverse bacterial growth in the water and in the substrate, which may cause disease. To prevent overfeeding, make sure that no food sinks to the aquarium floor before being eaten and that there is no leftover food on the surface after a few minutes. If this does happen, then you are feeding too much. (See previous advice for feeding bottom-dwelling fish.) Feed fish two or three times daily and in small quantities. Try to feed at regular intervals and spread the food evenly, so that all the fish get a chance to feed. Large fish may only need feeding once a day or even once every other day. For small fish, "little and often" is preferable.

***Above:** An automatic fish feeder can be used to deliver set quantities of food at regular intervals, allowing you to feed your fish when you go away for short periods.*

***Right:** The upturned mouth of the sailfin molly (Poecilia sphenops) makes feeding from the surface an easy task. Other species may feed at midwater level or from the aquarium floor.*

GROWING HEALTHY PLANTS

A healthy, thriving aquarium contains not only fish but, in most cases, plant life as well. Plants obtain all their food and energy from a combination of light and nutrients in the water; without either of these, they will not survive. This makes the correct water quality vital to the success of keeping aquarium plants, as well as fish.

Providing a balanced diet

To survive and grow in natural waters, plants utilize more than 18 trace elements in the form of mineral salts, as well as organic compounds. As we have seen in the natural water cycle shown on page 9, these trace elements are picked up as water passes through various layers of rock. Water that has passed through rock often reaches streams and rivers via natural springs that rise up through the ground. In nature, dense groupings of plant life can be found around these natural springs, because the water here is rich in mineral salts and trace elements. Plants also need organic compounds — the result of decomposing waste — to survive. Organic compounds are basically carbon atoms bound onto other elements. Plants are made up of roughly 50 percent carbon, so the availability of organic compounds is clearly vital for them.

Right: Both fish and plants rely on good water quality to thrive in the aquarium, although each has distinct, and sometimes differing, requirements. With a little prior thought and investment, combined with continuing good care, anyone can keep a healthy planted aquarium such as this one.

Obtaining nutrients

For plants to survive in the aquarium, it is not simply a matter of providing these nutrients and leaving the plants to it. Nutrients are found in two forms: bivalent and trivalent. Only the bivalent form is water soluble and can be used by plants. In water with oxygen levels above 2mg/liter, a bivalent nutrient such as iron (bivalent form, Fe_2) bonds with another iron atom (Fe) into a trivalent nutrient (Fe_3). The molecule is now too large to be absorbed by plants, rendering it useless. Many nutrient atoms have a tendency to bond together. During the bonding process an oxygen atom is used up, so effectively a bivalent nutrient is being "oxidized" into a trivalent one. Clearly, low oxygen levels would prevent this from happening, but most aquarium fish need oxygen levels higher than 2mg/liter. To solve this problem, use liquid plant fertilizers that contain substances called chelates. These organic compounds attach to bivalent nutrients and prevent them from oxidizing into the trivalent form. This allows nutrients to be available to plants in oxygen levels up to 8mg/liter. Above this level, chelates are destroyed. (Chelated fertilizers for garden plants help to make nutrients available in a similar way.)

The effects of high oxygen levels

Oxygen in water is vital for both fish and plants to respire and survive, but if levels are too high, it can become dangerous, especially for plants. High oxygen levels result in: the reduction of available nutrients by oxidation, which causes nutrient deficiency in both fish and plants; stress to fish that naturally live in low oxygen environments; and increased pH levels, making ammonia more toxic (see page 17).

How chelated nutrients are more efficient

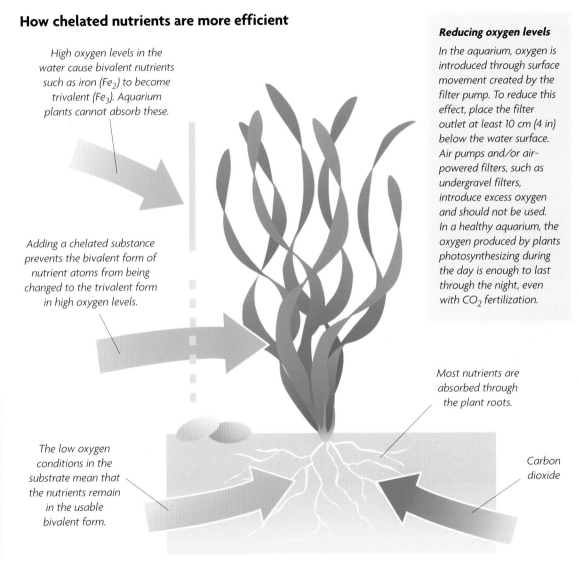

High oxygen levels in the water cause bivalent nutrients such as iron (Fe_2) to become trivalent (Fe_3). Aquarium plants cannot absorb these.

Adding a chelated substance prevents the bivalent form of nutrient atoms from being changed to the trivalent form in high oxygen levels.

The low oxygen conditions in the substrate mean that the nutrients remain in the usable bivalent form.

Reducing oxygen levels

In the aquarium, oxygen is introduced through surface movement created by the filter pump. To reduce this effect, place the filter outlet at least 10 cm (4 in) below the water surface. Air pumps and/or air-powered filters, such as undergravel filters, introduce excess oxygen and should not be used. In a healthy aquarium, the oxygen produced by plants photosynthesizing during the day is enough to last through the night, even with CO_2 fertilization.

Most nutrients are absorbed through the plant roots.

Carbon dioxide

Introducing carbon dioxide

Carbon dioxide (CO_2) is the most important nutrient for plants, considerably more than any other. Providing the required amount of CO_2 in the planted aquarium creates the difference between plants that thrive and those that merely survive.

As we have seen on page 15, CO_2 is constantly produced in the aquarium by the fish, plants, and also by the bacteria in the substrate and filter. However, in a well-planted aquarium the demand for CO_2 is more than the amount produced, so additional supplies are vitally important. The ideal level of CO_2 in a planted aquarium is about 35–45 mg/liter; at levels above 100mg/liter, damage can be caused to some fish. For larger aquariums, there are a number of systems available that will introduce CO_2 into the tank and maintain it at an ideal level. There are also cheaper systems that deliver CO_2 at a constant rate and provide enough for plants without saturating the aquarium. Whichever CO_2 system you choose, it is the best investment you can make to keep your plants healthy and growing strongly.

Providing a good substrate

Although not directly related to water quality, it is vital for plants to have a suitable substrate. The bacteria (releasing CO_2), organic compounds, and minerals within the substrate provide most of the nutrient requirements of plants, which they take up through their roots. In most aquariums, the substrate is simply a precleaned and washed gravel, containing virtually nothing of use to the plants. This is why most people cannot keep plants, despite the use of liquid fertilizers.

A good substrate should be at least 7.5 cm (3 in) deep, providing space for plants to spread their roots. A deep substrate also increases the likelihood of creating a low- or zero-oxygen layer. In zero-oxygen, nutrients are more easily available and this condition reflects the situation in nature, where aquatic plants root in anaerobic (no oxygen) substrate or mud. Although roots do need oxygen to thrive, this is provided from the plant's leaves growing above the substrate. Nutrients also have to be circulated through the substrate. The best way to do this is to install a low power heating cable in a winding pattern within the lowest part of the substrate (see page 47). The slightly warmer and cooler areas created between the turns of the heating cable circulate the nutrients slowly around the substrate.

How a CO$_2$ fertilization system works

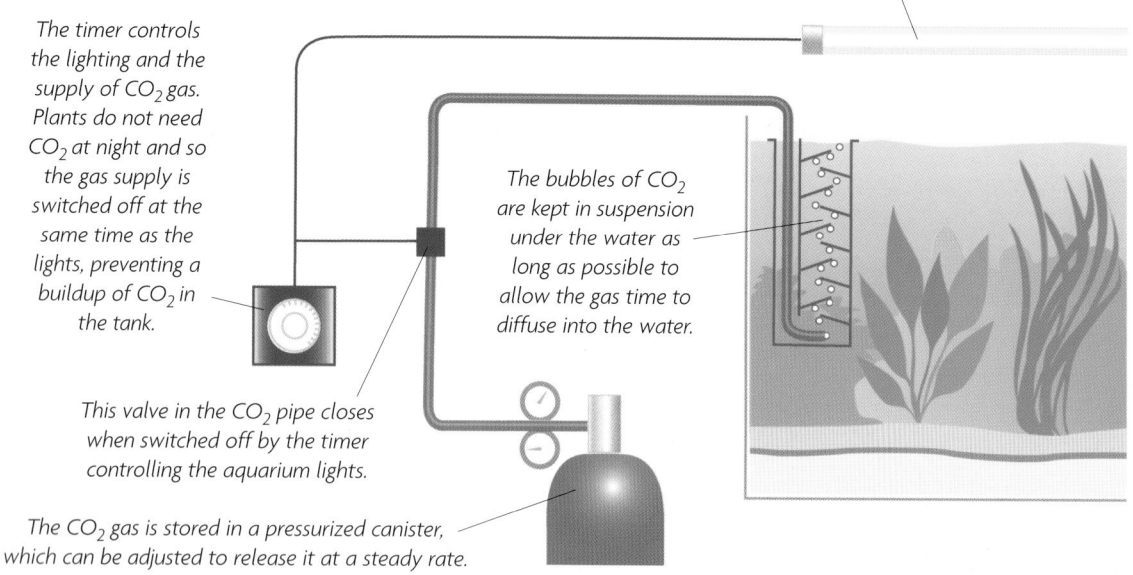

Aquarium lights provide the energy for photosynthesis.

The timer controls the lighting and the supply of CO_2 gas. Plants do not need CO_2 at night and so the gas supply is switched off at the same time as the lights, preventing a buildup of CO_2 in the tank.

The bubbles of CO_2 are kept in suspension under the water as long as possible to allow the gas time to diffuse into the water.

This valve in the CO_2 pipe closes when switched off by the timer controlling the aquarium lights.

The CO_2 gas is stored in a pressurized canister, which can be adjusted to release it at a steady rate.

Don't overdo it!

Do not be tempted to overfertilize to promote plant growth. Too many nutrients can damage plant life, as well as encourage algae.

Right: A school of harlequin rasboras (Rasbora heteromorpha) is ideal in an aquarium where fish and plants play an equal role in creating a stunning display.

An ideal substrate

A simple but effective substrate for plants would be, for example, from bottom to top: A heating cable covered with 5 cm (2 in) of fine lime-free gravel or sand, a nutrient-rich layer of either red tropical clay or a specifically designed planting substrate, and then a final 5 cm (2 in) layer of lime-free gravel (1–3 mm diameter).

Lime-free gravel is inert and does not affect water quality. As a planting substrate, it simply holds everything in place.

A thin layer of nutrient-rich substrate, such as this red clay-based material, releases nutrients slowly at a constant rate.

This silver sand compacts in the aquarium and contains little oxygen, ideal for holding bivalent nutrients that plants can use readily.

The heating cable creates a very slow moving circulation of water, carrying nutrients around the substrate.

To understand exactly how water quality affects the health of aquarium fish and why fish behave the way they do, you should look at the body of a fish and the physiological processes that allow it to survive in the aquatic environment. Fish contain many of the same organs as humans, carrying out the same functions – a heart pumping blood, a digestive system, a nervous system, eyes, brain, etc. There are also a few special adaptations that are a vital part of the fish's life beneath the water.

The immune system

Without an immune system, all animals, including humans, would quickly fall prey to the vast numbers of disease-causing pathogens that are encountered every day. Although nowhere near as effective as the immune systems of most mammals, fish have a number of defenses against disease and infection.

The best method of defense is prevention. This occurs at the fish's skin, where the scales embedded in the epidermis (the outer skin layer) form a shield against physical damage and prevent disease organisms from entering. The mucus coating contains natural fungicides and bactericides that help to kill any unwanted organisms. The mucus is constantly produced and renewed, so that any organisms that find their way into the mucus coating are likely to be discarded before they reach the body.

If any disease pathogens are swallowed, they are likely to receive an unwelcome reception in the fish's gut and intestinal tract, where conditions caused by digestive enzymes and a low pH (i.e., acidic) are unsuitable for most organisms. In the blood, white blood cells, along with specific antiviral and antibacterial chemicals, can be quickly transported to any areas harboring foreign intruders.

As a final defense, specific antigens are made in various parts of the body, mainly the spleen and kidney. Antigens are made to destroy disease pathogens "recognized" by the fish's body.

How water quality affects the immune system

As with humans, stress causes a fish's immune system to become less effective. Aquarium fish often endure high levels of stress before they settle in a permanent home. Transportation and a change of environment can be enough to stress already weak fish to the point where disease or environmental conditions become life threatening.

Any adverse water conditions can damage the immune system through stress, as will an incorrect physical environment and unsuitable tankmates. Pollutants such as ammonia and chlorine will strip the fish of mucus, leaving the body open to infection and damage. In many cases, adverse environmental conditions cause an immune response, such as increased production of mucus. This can often lead to respiratory problems, as the mucus interferes with the oxygen/carbon dioxide exchange, reducing the amount of available oxygen.

Osmosis and osmoregulation

Osmosis is the flow of water through a semi-permeable membrane from a dilute solution into a concentrated solution. A concentrated solution of water (containing many substances) will naturally "pull in" water from a more dilute solution (containing few substances), thus achieving a natural balance. Osmoregulation, therefore, is the regulation and control of this process. As with our own bodies, a fish's body is made up mainly of water. As the surrounding environment is also water, this means that osmosis occurs between the fish's body and its environment.

In fresh water, a fish's body contains a higher salt concentration than the surrounding environment. Due to the process of osmosis, the fish is constantly absorbing water from outside, mainly through the body and gills, and has to find a way of losing it. It does this by excreting large quantities of dilute urine, retaining as many salts as possible.

In marine fish, the surrounding environment has a higher salt concentration, so the process is reversed; the fish is constantly losing water from the body to the outside environment. To combat this effect,

Above: A severe infection of Saprolegnia *fungus, possibly caused by poor tank conditions, plus open wounds.*

Fish anatomy and basic physiology

The digestive and blood processing systems
The body cavity houses the following major organ systems that carry out vital functions.

Gut The gut chemically breaks down food matter and allows food materials to be absorbed into the body. Food is mainly digested in the intestine.

Pancreas Digestive enzymes are produced in the pancreas, which are then released into the intestine to break down food matter.

Spleen Red and white blood cells, important for transporting oxygen and for the fish's immune system, are produced and stored in the spleen.

Liver Old blood cells are broken down in the liver, producing bile, which is released as waste. The liver also stores glycogen, which is broken down into glucose as a source of energy.

Kidneys
The kidneys act as a "body filter," removing wastes picked up and transported by the bloodstream. Kidneys also regulate the salt and water content of the fish's body and control the production of ammonia-containing urea.

Swimbladder
This air-filled sac is used to regulate buoyancy in water. Not all fish have swimbladders; bottom-dwellers, such as many catfish, have no need to be buoyant, as they spend little time swimming in midwater.

Brain
The brain controls movement and bodily functions, as well as producing hormones. It also controls memory and intelligence.

Mouth
Water taken in through the mouth passes out over the gills.

Eyes
Most fish have wide-angle vision.

Dorsal fin

Gills
The thin membrane and large surface area of the gills allow oxygen from water, taken in through the mouth, to enter the bloodstream. Salts are absorbed through the gills by means of special chloride cells. The waste product, urea, is lost through the gills.

Adipose fin

Skeleton
The skeleton protects the internal organs and provides a supportive frame for the body.

Lateral line
The lateral line system helps the fish to locate its surroundings in relation to itself. Using vibrations and electric signals, it provides a "sixth sense."

Pectoral fins

Ventral, or pelvic, fins

Anal fin

Heart
The simple, four-chambered heart pumps blood around the body, creating a circulatory system that carries oxygen, nutrients, wastes, and hormones.

Caudal fin

marine fish effectively "drink" seawater, while filtering out salts and minerals and producing small amounts of highly concentrated urine.

Brackish water fish are able to adjust their osmoregulatory system depending on the salinity of the environment.

How water quality affects osmoregulation

A fish's osmoregulatory system is designed to match the conditions found in its natural environment. Soft water fish, such as discus and tetras, are accustomed to water with a relatively low salt content, so their osmoregulatory system is designed to retain as many salts as possible, vital for normal bodily functions. If the fish is placed in hard water, which typically contains high levels of calcium, it may not be able to remove enough of the excess calcium, since its osmoregulatory system is optimized to retain salts, rather than remove them. The excess calcium in the body is then deposited in the kidneys, causing damage and further reducing the kidneys' ability to remove substances.

The osmoregulatory system in fish that are accustomed to hard water with a high calcium and mineral content need not be as efficient as that of soft water fish, as salts are more readily available. However, when placed in soft water, these fish may not be able to obtain enough salts from their environment, causing physiological problems.

Toxic ammonia in the water also affects osmosis by increasing the permeability of the gills and body, increasing the flow of water through the body, and allowing a loss of salts.

Adding salt to reduce osmotic stress

During times of damage, disease, or recovery, it can be beneficial to add a small quantity of salt to the freshwater aquarium. By reducing the difference in salt concentration between the fish's body and its environment, the "osmotic stress" placed upon the fish is reduced and it can concentrate more energy on recovery. For freshwater fish, add about 1gm of salt per liter of water in the aquarium (1.6 oz per 10 gallons).

How the gills work

As with all animals, fish require oxygen to live. The process by which oxygen is obtained is called respiration. Water contains a far lower concentration of oxygen than is found in air, so fish have had to develop a very efficient way of extracting as much oxygen as possible from their environment. Just as you absorb oxygen into your blood through your lungs, fish absorb oxygen from the water through their gills. The gills are made up of a very thin membrane over which water is passed. The blood in

Osmoregulation in a freshwater fish

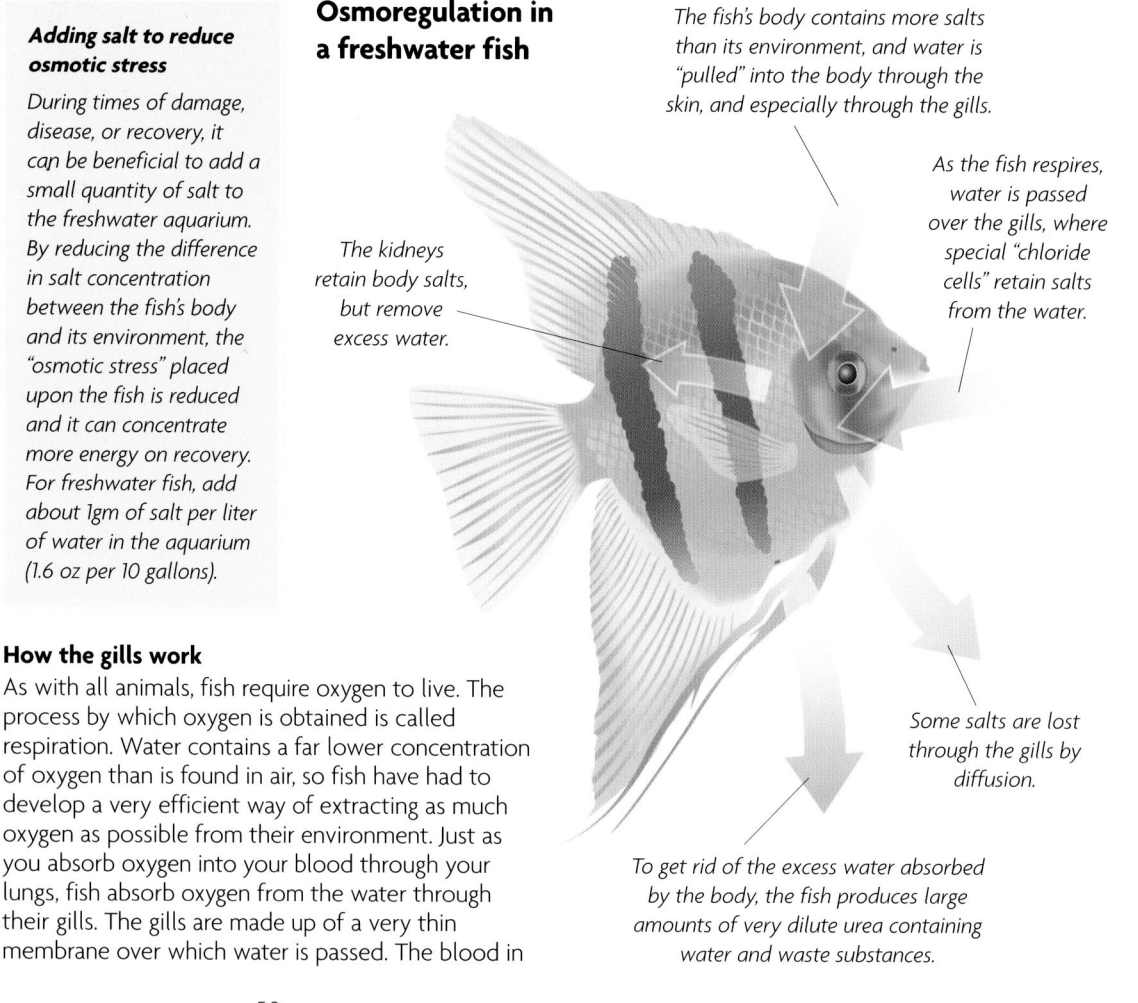

The fish's body contains more salts than its environment, and water is "pulled" into the body through the skin, and especially through the gills.

As the fish respires, water is passed over the gills, where special "chloride cells" retain salts from the water.

The kidneys retain body salts, but remove excess water.

Some salts are lost through the gills by diffusion.

To get rid of the excess water absorbed by the body, the fish produces large amounts of very dilute urea containing water and waste substances.

the gills is low in oxygen, so by a process of diffusion, oxygen passes into the blood through the gill membrane from the surrounding water.

Due to the thin membrane of the gills, a large amount of water is taken into the body by osmosis, which has to be excreted as urine. The gills contain special chloride cells that retain salts in the body, while allowing water to pass through the body.

How water quality affects the gills

The gills of a fish are very delicate and, due to their exposed nature, are very susceptible to problems related to adverse water quality. The main cause of gill-related problems in aquarium fish is the use of untreated tap water and the dangerous levels of chlorine found in tap water. Chlorine actively destroys the gill membrane and strips away the protective mucus. The fish's immune response results in abnormal cell growth around the gills, which restricts oxygen absorption. Ammonia causes the same problems, stripping away mucus from the gills, which causes them to swell and obstruct water flow. In an environment that is too alkaline, the same problem occurs. If the environment is too acidic for the fish, then excess mucus is produced and iron is also deposited on the gills, giving them a grayish appearance.

Blood circulation

A fish's circulation is an internal transport system in which nutrients, wastes, and oxygen are constantly transported around the body. Blood is the medium that transports useful oxygen, nutrients, and hormones to cells throughout the body, and removes waste carbon dioxide and toxins. It is made up of plasma, red blood cells, and white blood cells. Plasma is a watery fluid that carries salts, waste matter, and glucose for energy. The red blood cells contain hemoglobin, a substance that binds with oxygen and carries it to cells and tissues, where it is exchanged for waste carbon dioxide. The white blood cells form the main immune defense within the body and congregate around infected, inflamed, or damaged areas of the body. The white blood cells then help to destroy and remove bacterial and viral infection, as well as contribute to the repair of damaged tissue.

How water quality affects blood

Most chemicals introduced to the aquarium will be easily passed through the gill membrane, or otherwise be absorbed by the fish's body, and end up in the blood system. This allows chemicals to pass throughout the fish's body, which is useful in the case of medication, but not where harmful toxins are concerned. The red blood cells and their ability to carry oxygen are most affected by adverse water quality. Toxic nitrite in the blood breaks down the red blood cells and oxidize iron in hemoglobin, turning it into methemoglobin, which is unable to carry oxygen. This effect is visible, because the blood and gill tissue may turn a brown color. Ammonia also impairs the ability of hemoglobin to carry oxygen, causing oxygen deficiency.

Water keeping is the key

The osmoregulatory system, immune system, gills, and blood are the systems most commonly influenced by adverse water quality, but the whole body is affected by its environment. Water quality directly influences the fish's physical health in almost every way, which is why it is vital to maintain correct water quality. Fishkeeping is more a case of "water-keeping" than anything else. In the right environment, the fish more than take care of themselves.

Left: The gills are made up of thin filaments, richly supplied with blood capillaries. As water passes over and around them, oxygen diffuses from the water into the tiny blood vessels lying close to the surface. Carbon dioxide and other waste materials pass from the blood into the water. To make these exchanges more efficient, the blood in the capillaries flows in the opposite direction to the water.

As we have seen, water quality directly affects the aquarium and the health of the fish. There are also a number of related adverse effects that can be caused by conditions within the aquarium. Unfavorable water quality can cause algae to bloom and a host of aquatic diseases to thrive, while pests such as snails damage plants and look less than attractive.

Algae in the aquarium

Despite the best care, there are always forms of algae that can affect the aquarium. Algae grow wherever there is light and a food source, both of which are always present in the aquarium. Heavy planting helps to reduce the occurrence of all forms of algae by using up nutrients and light.

Algae are a simple, primitive form of aquatic plant that either grow on substrates and solid objects, or are found "free-floating" in the water. A small amount of algae is perfectly normal and can even add to the overall "natural" appearance of rocks and substrates, but when it grows out of control, the effect is, at best, undesirable. Given the chance, problem algae choke plants, reduce oxygen to dangerous levels, and can affect water quality to such a degree that fish may die. As a general preventative, add a few algae-eating fish, such as loaches or catfish, to the tank. Good water quality and correct lighting should prevent most algal blooms. Avoid using fertilizers for a few weeks until plants are established. They use nutrients mainly for growth and reproduction, which only occurs when they are established and healthy. If fertilizers are used too early, there will be an excess of nutrients in the water.

Algae in new aquariums

Algal blooms often occur in newly set up aquariums because of fluctuations in water quality. These blooms should clear fairly quickly and need not be a cause for undue concern.

Above: Algae use up a great deal of oxygen and, in turn, produce a mass of carbon dioxide, as can be seen here. If algae are not kept in check, oxygen levels in the aquarium can be reduced to dangerous levels.

Right: Remove algae from the front glass using an algae pad or scraper. Providing algae growth is not too rapid, you need not clean the rear and side panels, leaving food for algae-eating fish. Make sure the algae pad is only used in the aquarium and is designed for that purpose. Domestic cleaning pads often contain chemicals that may be harmful in the aquarium.

Single-celled algae

If the water turns a green color, it is likely to be as a result of single-celled algae that arise if there is too much light (almost always sunlight) and excess organic matter, such as uneaten food. There are a number of chemical treatments available to kill single-celled algae, but it is always best to remove the cause of the problem, rather than treat the aquarium with unnecessary chemicals. Reduce the amount of light reaching the aquarium and keep a careful check on feeding. Changing the water does not help, as the fresh, new water simply encourages the algae to bloom again.

Filamentous algae

These fibrous algae, also known as thread algae, hair algae, and blanketweed, cover plants and decor, causing an unsightly problem that is hard to eradicate. Again, excess or incorrect lighting,

Right: This algae-eating catfish (Ancistrus dolichopterus) makes a useful addition to a community aquarium, spending its time grazing algae from the aquarium glass, plants, and decor. Make sure bogwood is available, as it forms a natural part of the fish's diet.

Below: Unsightly filamentous algae are commonly found as blanketweed in garden ponds. In the aquarium, they can quickly choke plants and cause water quality problems.

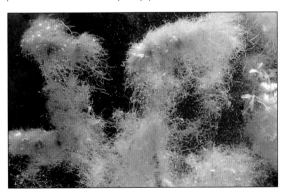

combined with excess organic matter, may cause this type of algae to bloom. The best solution is to remove physically as much algae as possible and follow this with a thorough gravel clean (page 39).

Blue-green algae

These algae form a thin blanket across any surface. They feel slimy and have a distinctive smell that emanates from the water. Blue-green algae are often caused by high nutrient levels and bad water quality. They are easy to remove with a siphon, but quickly regrow. Virtually no algae-eating fish eat blue-green algae. Occasionally, a different form of blue-green algae can be seen in the aquarium as surface scum.

Brown algae

Although often called brown algae, these are not part of the true brown algae, which are found in seawater. These algae grow on the aquarium glass and, providing it is cleaned off regularly, do not cause a problem. Simply wipe it off with a suitable aquarium cleaning pad. Brown algae often occur in aquariums with hard water or low light levels.

Removing dead algae

Algal blooms can naturally die back quite quickly once certain nutrients are exhausted. Be sure to remove all the dead algae, otherwise they will pollute the water.

Brush algae

Usually found on plant leaves or bogwood, brush algae consist of small, black or brown furlike tufts, no more than 1 cm (0.4 in) high. There are no special conditions that encourage them to grow, but once established, they slowly spread and become unsightly. The only remedy is to remove completely any objects on which the algae have settled.

Snails in the aquarium

Snails may enter the aquarium environment via a number of routes and can quickly become a problem. Many breed very quickly and prove hard to get rid of. They become unsightly and act as carriers for some diseases. Dead snails pollute the water. The most common route for snails to enter the aquarium is via live plants. Today, the plants available from most retailers are generally free of snails, but one or two of these pests always escape detection and if you are unlucky, they may end up in your tank. Before you put them in the aquarium, thoroughly check any plants you buy for snails. You can buy a chemical "dip" for aquarium plants that kills any snails. Use it before adding the plants to the tank.

Also, avoid introducing plants from ponds or other outside sources. You may introduce not only snails, but also aquatic diseases and other pests.

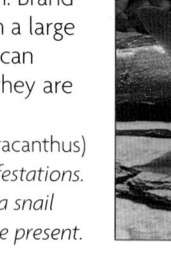

Just a single snail could be the start of a widespread problem and should be removed immediately.

Controlling snail populations

Occasionally, snails can be kept in the aquarium without becoming a problem. In this case they may be useful, moving substrate around and removing waste organic matter and algae. To control their breeding, reduce the amount of organic waste in the aquarium by regular gravel cleaning.

At night, many snails gather along the aquarium glass and are easy to remove. Another trick is to place a saucer upside down in the center of the tank with a few food pellets or tablets underneath. Most fish, excluding a few loaches and catfish, are unable to get under the saucer, but the food is a lure for the snail population. After a few hours, the snails will have collected underneath the saucer and can be removed.

Removing snail populations

Snails are notoriously difficult to eradicate and some methods of removal are more damaging to the aquarium environment than the snails themselves. Chemical treatments are available, but should be used with extreme caution. Brand-name snail killers can result in a large number of snail corpses that can pollute the aquarium unless they are

Right: Clown loaches (Botia macracanthus) are a natural solution to snail infestations. Do not treat the aquarium with a snail killer when these sensitive fish are present.

all removed – and it is usually almost impossible to find and remove them all. Snail flesh is very high in protein which, when it decomposes, results in high ammonia and nitrite levels, both toxic to fish. Snail killers are often based on metals that are dangerous to some delicate fish, can adversely affect and even kill some plants, and are also neutralized by water conditioners, making them ineffective. In any case, most currently available snail killers are unlikely to kill the entire population and the remaining snails will breed quickly. Snail eggs also are rarely affected by most snail killers.

The best method of eradicating snails is simply to remove them physically whenever you see them. There are also some fish that will eat snails and they, combined with physical removal, are usually enough

to remove all the snails. A good example is the clown loach which, even when small, will eat snails as they hatch, leaving the fishkeeper to remove the larger, more visible ones.

Diseases

There are countless diseases that can affect aquarium fish and it is almost certain that you will encounter a few of the common ones, whether in a mild or more severe form. With the correct preventative care and quick diagnosis and treatment, disease should rarely strike and is easy to eradicate. The key to controlling disease is speed; quickly establish and remove the cause of the problem, and then apply an effective and suitable treatment.

Like other animals, fish have an immune system designed to prevent disease from taking hold (see page 48). If the immune system is compromised in any way – for example, through bad water quality – then the fish is laid open to a whole array of aquatic diseases. In severe cases of bad or incorrect water quality, fish may exhibit obvious reactions, even before other diseases have a chance to affect the fish, and these conditions can be described as environmental disease. Symptoms include gasping or increased respiration, loss of color, listlessness, an excess or a lack of mucus, sores on the body, discolored gills, erratic behavior, and jumping. The most extreme reaction to environmental disease is death, which will occur in a number of fish, regardless of the species involved.

Environmental diseases

Acidosis; Alkalosis; Gas bubble disease; Metal and chemical toxicity; Poisoning by ammonia, chlorine, and nitrite, or household cleaners and insecticides

Below: This fish is showing signs of finrot, often caused by bad water quality. Use a suitable treatment and increase the frequency of water changes. When signs of environmental disease appear, check water quality and take steps to improve tank maintenance (see pages 38–41).

A natural defense

Fish constantly produce a mucus layer around the body and this is what gives them a "slimy" feel. The mucus is produced mainly to stop diseases from entering the body. As the mucus is continually produced and discarded, any disease pathogens present on the body surface are eliminated along with the mucus. If fish produce more mucus than normal, it may be a sign either of bad environmental conditions, or of disease.

Prevention and treatment

Maintaining good filtration, carrying out regular tank maintenance, providing the correct water quality for the species you keep, and regular water testing will prevent environmental diseases. But what if things do go wrong? Depending on the severity of the adverse environmental conditions, there are a number of treatments. In any case, the first step is to aerate the water immediately. This allows gases to escape and increases the availability of oxygen. Follow this with comprehensive water testing to discover the cause of the problem, and carry out a 25–30 percent water change. In severe cases, it may be necessary to change almost all the water, providing you have an available source of heated, dechlorinated water. Adding a chemical medium, such as activated carbon, helps to remove pollutants. Poisoning by external chemicals may require a complete change of tank while you empty and thoroughly clean the affected one.

Follow directions

Do not be tempted to increase the dosage. Many treatments can be harmful if overdosed. Never mix treatments unless this is recommended by the manufacturer. Many of them recommend redosing after a set period if a fish has not recovered. If you do this, follow the instructions.

Using treatments

When treating sick fish, it is vital that suitable treatments are correctly administered. This is in addition to providing the correct water quality and environment. There are specific treatments for different types of disease (bacterial, fungal, and so on) and for individual diseases, but there are a few steps you must take with most treatments to ensure they are used to the best effect.

Before treating

To get the most from any treatment, make sure that the aquarium environment is in the best possible condition. An additional water change (about 25 percent), gravel clean, and filter maintenance will all help to provide a stable environment. Remove any carbon or other chemical medium from the filter, plus any excess organic waste, as both of these will absorb the medication, rendering it useless. If necessary, add additional aeration via an air pump and airstone.

Left: Many symptoms of disease, combined with the use of disease medications, reduce the amount of oxygen available to the fish. Introduce additional aeration using a suitable air pump.

The "hospital" tank

In some cases, it may be worth setting up a separate aquarium to treat fish, especially if only one or two are affected. A hospital, or treatment, tank can be fairly basic as it need not be aesthetically pleasing. Substrate is not necessary, but the fish may appreciate a thin layer of dark or black gravel. Add a few rocks, clay plant pots and plastic plants as hiding places. Lighting is not necessary and it may help the fish's recovery if they are kept in subdued light. Filtration can be provided by a small internal filter or air-powered sponge filter. Provide additional aeration through an airstone and air pump. Any equipment, such as nets or cleaning pads, should be kept separate from the main aquarium to reduce the risk of transferring disease pathogens.

In addition to serving as a hospital tank, this setup could be used for quarantining fish, separating troublesome fish, or even as a breeding tank.

Preparing treatments

To avoid undue stress, it may be worth mixing treatments with water in a separate container before introducing the mixture to the aquarium.

Dosage

Most medications are administered either in a single dose or as a course of treatment over a set period of time. Whatever the dosage rate, follow it accurately and complete the whole course of treatment, even if the fish's symptoms disappear. Many diseases, such as whitespot, may reappear if the whole course of treatment is not completed.

Treating

Although treatments are designed to aid recovery and kill disease pathogens, many of them cause damage to the fish's body, so treatment and recovery can be very stressful. Give the fish special care while they are being treated. Increase the number of feeds per day (but not the amount of food). It may be worth feeding high protein, live, or frozen foods instead of the fish's normal diet, as the additional protein will help the fish to repair itself. Also increase the frequency of water changes. For example, instead of a 20 percent change each week, carry out a 10 percent change every other day. If possible, reduce the lighting and/or place a cover over the front of the aquarium so that fish are not frightened by people passing by or peering in. You can increase aeration for the duration of the treatment.

1 Carefully measure out the correct amount of treatment, or the number of drops recommended, and add this to a jug of water taken from the aquarium.

Calculating aquarium capacity

The amount of medication required is usually based on the volume of the aquarium in liters or gallons.
To work out the capacity of your aquarium in liters multiply the length, depth and width of the aquarium in centimeters (e.g., 60x30x30 = 54000) and divide this figure by 1000 (54000 ÷ 1000 = 54 liters). To convert to gallons, multiply this figure by 0.22.

2 Mix the treatment into the water in the jug. Make sure that the spoon or other implement you use to mix the treatment is clean and free from any chemicals.

3 Slowly pour the treatment over the surface of the aquarium. Diluting the mixture in this way ensures an even distribution of the medication throughout the tank.

Biological filtration

Many aquarium treatments are harmful to filter bacteria, hindering the biological filtration process. If this is the case, then maintain good water quality by increasing the frequency of water changes.

The natural water cycle on page 9 shows how water quality is modified by the soil, vegetation, and rocks over and through which it flows. In nature, geologically differing areas contribute a variety of changes to the water chemistry of streams, lakes, and rivers. Aquarium fish are found in these bodies of freshwater all over the world, and in many different habitats. They adapt to survive in specific environments, so to keep aquarium fish successfully, you must try to re-create their natural habitat, in terms of their physical and chemical environments. To understand their requirements, first look at some of their natural habitats.

Lake Malawi fish, such as this zebra cichlid (Pseudotropheus sp.), often exhibit stunning coloration. Re-creating their natural environment and water quality in the aquarium will show them at their best.

LAKE MALAWI

The best known rift lake in fishkeeping is Lake Malawi. At more than 600 km (375 miles) long and more than 700 m (2296 ft) deep in places, it is the ninth largest lake in the world, and more of a freshwater ocean than a lake. Because it contains such a massive amount of fresh water, the water chemistry and conditions remain relatively stable. Any pollutants entering the lake, either man-made or in the form of organic waste from fish, are simply diluted in the mass of water. However, pollutants from life within the lake are relatively small. With no river flowing into it and only one outlet, the lake has had little aquatic life introduced to it and remains fairly isolated. But there are more than 600 species of fish – the Malawi cichlids – that feed primarily off algae and the tiny

Above: *This barren aquascape is typical of Lake Malawi's rocky habitat. Apart from the fish, there is little aquatic life to be seen. In the aquarium, the natural water quality of the lake is easy to reproduce.*

organisms that live within them. There are also invertebrate feeders and almost as many fish-eating cichlids in Lake Malawi as there are algal grazers.

Rocks and waves raise the pH

The rock around the lake and past volcanic activity releasing mineral ions, combined with comparatively little organic life, give the water a high pH level of between 7.5 and 8.5. The high pH level can be seen particularly in the shallows, where most fish are found. Wave action in the shallows increases the gas exchange between the water and the air, allowing carbon dioxide to escape. The reduction of carbon dioxide in the water causes less carbonic acid to be produced, so there is little acidic organic substance in the water to keep pH levels down.

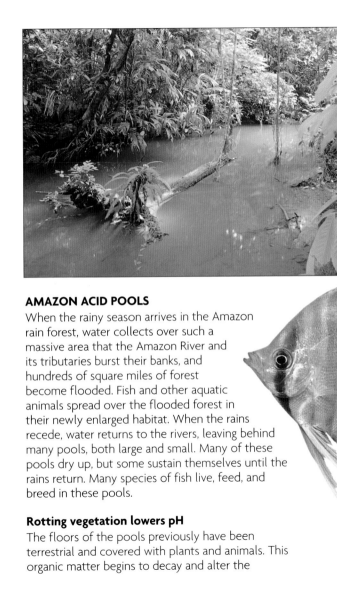

AMAZON ACID POOLS

When the rainy season arrives in the Amazon rain forest, water collects over such a massive area that the Amazon River and its tributaries burst their banks, and hundreds of square miles of forest become flooded. Fish and other aquatic animals spread over the flooded forest in their newly enlarged habitat. When the rains recede, water returns to the rivers, leaving behind many pools, both large and small. Many of these pools dry up, but some sustain themselves until the rains return. Many species of fish live, feed, and breed in these pools.

Rotting vegetation lowers pH

The floors of the pools previously have been terrestrial and covered with plants and animals. This organic matter begins to decay and alter the chemistry of the pool. The waste material and rotting vegetation release humic acids, staining the water the color of tea. Bacteria, and other organisms feeding from this dead matter, release carbon dioxide, producing carbonic acid. The humic and carbonic acids released in the small body of water causes a substantial drop in pH levels. It is not uncommon for the pH level to drop to as low as 4 or 5 in this environment.

In the heat of the moment

If the pool is devoid of overhanging vegetation, direct sunlight may cause the water temperature to become unusually high, often above 33°C (93°F). In this low pH, high temperature environment, many fish do not survive, but some positively enjoy it. For some fish it is the ideal breeding environment; dead organic matter allows many small food sources, such as microalgae and infusoria, to appear and a lack of aquatic predators provides a good place to raise young fry.

SWAMP LIFE

Over large areas of flat land, with impermeable rock or clay not far beneath the ground, and little overhead vegetation, swamps may be formed. A lack of overhead vegetation and a shallow body of water, combined with a fertile substrate and plenty of sunlight, creates the ideal environment for aquatic and water-loving vegetation to thrive. In swamps, the aquatic vegetation is so densely packed that the water flow is reduced to virtually nothing.

Suffocating conditions

This underwater jungle has many effects on the water chemistry of the swamps. Oxygen levels are drastically reduced, and the air/water gas exchange is hindered both by the slow water flow and by aquatic plants covering most of the water surface. Respiration from plants, fish, and organisms feeding off the waste organic matter uses up any oxygen left in the water. Consequently, carbon dioxide is produced in vast amounts through respiration. The carbon dioxide acts as a food source for plants and also produces carbonic acid, lowering the pH levels. As plants also use up minerals as food, the hardness level of the swamps drops to only a few degrees, reducing the water's buffering capacity – the ability to resist pH changes.

Just another day in the swamp

Through photosynthesis and respiration, the plants produce oxygen during the day and carbon dioxide at night. As both oxygen and carbon dioxide levels affect pH, there are large fluctuations in pH during a 24-hour period. To make things worse, the swamp – covering a large area, with little water movement, and shallow depth – heats up quickly in the daytime sun and cools at night. Fish can adapt and evolve to cope with daily temperature and pH fluctuations, but coping with almost no oxygen is a little trickier. Of the fish found in swamps and low oxygen areas, the most commonly seen in fishkeeping are the gouramis,

This juvenile scat (Scatophagus argus) is found in estuaries. As it gets older, it will spend more time in the ocean.

part of the Anabantid group of fish. Anabantids possess a unique air-breathing organ called the labyrinth organ, which allows them to take air from the atmosphere and absorb oxygen into the body.

BRACKISH WATERS

As the river reaches the last leg of its journey, it eventually flows into the ocean, and it is here that you find brackish waters. In larger rivers, the point where freshwater ends and saltwater begins is indistinct, and variations in salinity occur over many miles.

Below: In the brackish environment, conditions are harsh and constantly changing. Many fish can be found both in the brackish river and along the shoreline. The habitat in this picture is a haven for birds, fish, and other animals.

When the tide is out, freshwater extends further toward the sea, but when the tide comes in, saline water travels upriver for many miles. Many fish cannot tolerate the constantly changing salt conditions, but some have adapted to cope with the daily fluctuations. While some fish move with these daily fluctuations, staying in water with the same salinity, others simply adjust to the changes. The reason why fish and other animals have learned to live in this hostile, changing environment is because it is rich in organic matter and, therefore, food sources. All the organic matter and sediments picked up by the river on its journey are deposited here and in the ocean. Numerous bacteria, fungi, and microorganisms feed off the rich sediment, and in turn provide food for shrimps and fish.

AUSTRALIAN POOLS AND RIVERS

Apart from a few permanent waterways and rivers, the habitats of many Australian fish change from year to year. Heavy monsoon rains occur in some areas during the summer months and leave behind many pools and waterholes that contain communities of tropical fish. Due to the varying nature of the landscape and rock work, conditions in these pools and waterholes can change dramatically. Most Australian fish can cope with temperatures in the 15–35°C (59–95°F) range. The desert goby *(Chlamydogobius eremius)* may be able to survive in water temperatures of 4–42°C (39–104°F) for short periods of time. Many water bodies can become brackish very quickly, and the fish that inhabit these waters can cope with almost instant changes in salinity by as much as 15ppt. With little aquatic life in some pools, and surrounding rock of chalk and limestone, some areas exhibit pH levels as high as 9.5. In contrast, some rainbowfish come from areas with an acidic pH level of 5.0

CENTRAL AMERICAN RIVERS

The Central American landscape is a rocky, mountainous area, and the rivers here are relatively short from source to mouth. The landscape creates fast flowing rivers, which become raging torrents in the rainy season. This fast water movement erodes much underlying soil, leaving a bed of rocks and gravel substrate. Calcareous limestone rock is found in many parts of Central America and minerals picked up from these rocks cause the water's pH to rise as high as 8.5. The combination of calcareous limestone and a lack of organic matter results in hard and alkaline river water.

Simulating habitats in the aquarium

These are just a few examples of some of the natural habitats in which aquarium fish can be found. Just by looking at the different natural habitats, you can see what effect water quality has on the lives of the fish.

In the aquarium, the extremes of water quality found in some habitats do not have to be re-created exactly. However, it is important that the aquarium becomes a comfortable environment, with water quality close to that found in nature. For example, gouramis do not have to be kept in water with little oxygen, but they do benefit from dense planting and hiding places such as they would find in the wild.

Similarly, brackish water fish do not have to experience daily fluctuations in salinity, but they do need some salt added to the aquarium. Now we will look at how to provide the correct environment in the aquarium for your fish to thrive.

Left: This overhead view of a Central American river shows the exposed bedrock from which salts and minerals are released into the water, often raising pH and hardness levels.

The territorial and destructive Jack Dempsey (Herichthys octofasciatus) *from Central America makes an excellent specimen fish.*

61

By understanding their natural environment and how to re-create it in the aquarium, you can ensure that your fish stay healthy. Water quality is by far the most important factor in creating a suitable environment, but providing the physical surroundings and tank decor to suit the fish's needs is just as important. Most fish can be grouped into certain categories with regard to decor and water quality. Individual species within a group may be the exception to the rule, so the following is a guideline only.

Livebearers

In nature, livebearers share the same geographical area as the large Central American cichlids. However, the livebearers are more likely to be found in the smaller streams, backwaters, and pools than in the main rivers. Smaller bodies of water are more prone to fluctuations in water quality and the livebearers have become a hardy group of fish, ideal for the beginner aquarist. Commonly known livebearers include guppies, mollies, platies, and swordtails.

The soil and rock in their natural habitat is often calcareous, so the livebearers require harder water, with a pH of 7.8–8.5. Some species tolerate water with a pH as low as 7. Keep hardness levels above 12°dGH. In the wild, many livebearers can be found in brackish environments and may tolerate the addition of salt to the aquarium. Ensure that the rest of the aquarium population tolerates salt as well. Many varieties now available need warmth; keep them at about 26–28°C (79–82°F). Provide hiding places in the form of hardy plants, such as *Vallisneria*, *Microsorium*, *Sagittaria*, and *Hygrophila*.

Right: The platy (Xiphophorus maculatus) makes an excellent addition to the community aquarium and is available in many different color types. It is peaceful, small, and breeds easily.

Below: Only the male swordtail (Xiphophorus helleri) has the swordlike caudal fin. This fish shows the natural coloration found in the wild.

Ideal conditions

pH / Hardness: 7.8-8.5 / 12-30°dGH.
Temperature: 20-28°C (68-82°F). Some tank-bred varieties at no less than 26°C (79°F).
Food: Flake, live foods, and algae.
Stocking: Keep in schools of three or more; twice as many females as males.
Minimum tank size: 60 cm (24 in).
Environment: Clear water, moderate current, open swimming spaces, and planting around sides and rear.

The common zebra danio *(Brachydanio rerio)* is very popular and an ideal starter fish since it tolerates short term nitrite fluctuations. Other common danios include the Bengal danio *(Danio devario)* and the giant danio *(Danio malabaricus).* With the exception of the smaller barbs (see page 64), both danios and barbs are open water swimmers and enjoy clean, clear, moving water. Most barbs are not fussy with regard to pH and hardness levels, but may prefer slightly lower temperatures. In the aquarium, they are constantly active and need large, open swimming areas. Despite their apparent confidence, many barbs are also quite timid and shy and should be provided with hiding places around the back and sides of the tank. Being school fish, you should always keep them in groups of six or more.

Ideal conditions

pH / Hardness: 6.5-7.5 / 7-15°dGH.
Temperature: 23-26°C (73-79°F).
Food: Flake, bloodworm, regular live foods.
Stocking: Groups of six or more.
Minimum tank size: 75 cm (30 in), depending on species.
Environment: Clean, clear, oxygenated water, strong current, open swimming spaces, dark caves, and hiding areas with little water movement.

Above: *The zebra danio (Brachydanio rerio), is constantly active in the aquarium, so much so, that they may stress slower moving, timid fish. Danios are an excellent beginner species.*

Left: *The Bengal danio (Danio devario) can be found in flooded habitats of northern India. In common with many barbs, it is a temperate fish and can be kept in unheated indoor aquariums.*

Above: *This fish is a gold, tank-bred variety of the zebra danio. Long-finned and leopard varieties are also available. These fish are midwater feeders and appreciate live foods such as daphnia.*

The majority of common aquarium fish are tetras and small barbs. These small, school fish are generally peaceful, not demanding, and ideal for most beginners. In the wild, tetras can be found in the Amazon River system, where the water is often soft and acidic. They live along the river banks, hiding among roots and wood, searching for small aquatic animals, and fruits and seeds from overhanging vegetation. Although there is much organic debris and a rich variety of life within their natural habitat, levels of nitrites and ammonia are virtually always zero due to constant bacterial action within the river.

Small barbs, such as the common tiger barb *(Barbus tetrazona)*, are found in many habitats worldwide, although not often in the Amazon system. They inhabit slow-moving waters and can be found among plant growth along the banks of streams and rivers. Although tetras and barbs are found in different areas, they enjoy the same type of habitat and water quality. Acidic water, with low to medium hardness and few pollutants, is ideal. Provide plant growth for these fish to hide in and a dark substrate that mimics their natural habitat.

Right: The cardinal tetra (Paracheirodon axelrodi) *exhibits stunning red and blue coloration. These fish do not survive well in hard water, but if kept in large groups in soft water, they become brilliant aquarium fish.*

Below: These tiger barbs (Barbus tetrazona) *appreciate open swimming spaces. Tiger barbs have a reputation as fin nippers, but if kept in groups of six or more, this habit can be curbed.*

Left: *The black neon (Hyphessobrycon herbertaxelrodi) has a robust appearance and makes an ideal community fish. Many tetras, such as the black neon, prefer subdued light and a dark substrate.*

Left: *This ruby barb (Barbus nigrofasciatus) comes from slow-moving streams, often with overhanging vegetation. It becomes skittish if kept in bright light. Males of this species exhibit stunning coloration.*

Below: *Megalamphodus megalopterus, the black phantom tetra, is not as demanding in terms of water quality as many other tetras, but appreciates a little cover or shade. It is a comical and beautiful little fish.*

Ideal conditions

pH / Hardness: 5.5-7 / 5-10°dGH.
Temperature: 23-27°C (73-80°F).
Food: Flake, bloodworm, daphnia, live foods.
Stocking: Groups of six or more.
Minimum tank size: 60 cm (24 in).
Environment: Subdued light, shading or dark caves are important. Gentle water movement, dark substrate, plants, and bogwood.

Many gouramis come from the dense swamp areas of Indonesia and are accustomed to densely planted dark areas, with little oxygen or water movement. This can be re-created in the aquarium with bogwood and heavy planting. The fish are also used to slightly acidic water and adding carbon dioxide will help, both as a plant fertilizer and to keep pH levels acidic. In the aquarium, the fish are not be bothered by strong light, providing they have a few shelters. Ideally, provide a few floating plants or plants with large leaves, such as the tiger lilies, as cover. A dark substrate also helps to make the fish feel at home and shows off their colors. Gouramis can be shy, so do not mix them with very active fish, such as some barbs and danios. Most gouramis are peaceful, but males of some species can be aggressive.

Ideal conditions

pH / Hardness: 6-7.5 / 5-20°dGH.
Temperature: 24-28°C (75-82°F).
Food: Flake, bloodworm, daphnia and live foods.
Stocking: In pairs, singles, or groups, depending on species.
Minimum tank size: 60 cm (24 in).
Environment: Very little water movement, dense planting to provide cover and shade.

Right: The male dwarf gourami (Colisa lalia) has wonderful coloration, but the female has almost none. A peaceful fish.

Left: The three-spot gourami (Trichogaster trichopterus) is very hardy, not fussy about pH levels, and can be kept in hard water. Males fight and more than one should only be kept among large groups of ten or more.

Right: The male Siamese fighting fish (Betta splendens) has stunning finnage that will be nipped at by barbs, tetras, and other fish. Do not keep two males together; they will fight until one is dead.

As with other cichlids, the Lake Malawi cichlids are especially territorial and aggressive toward each other. This can be combated by densely stocking the fish, thus eliminating the chances of territories being formed. Given dense stocking levels and the fish's messy feeding habits, the waste production in the aquarium is increased. It is important to use a good method of filtration in the aquarium – ideally an oversized external filter.

In their natural habitat, there are many rocks in which the fish can hide from predators and aggressive individuals. This must also be re-created in the aquarium. Build up rockwork against the entire back and sides of the aquarium, leaving numerous holes and caves as hiding places. To keep pH levels high, you can use calcium-based rocks, such as tufa or ocean rock, in the aquarium. If the pH drops, these rocks will release calcium into the water, acting as a buffer and raising the hardness and pH. Increased surface agitation also allows carbon dioxide to escape, preventing drops in pH. Remember that water chemistry is very stable in the lake, so fluctuations in water chemistry in the aquarium are not favorable to the fish.

Right: In the wild, this yellow variety of Cynotilapia afra *feeds in open waters near to the shore. In the aquarium, it needs plenty of hiding places close by.*

Above: Sciaenochromis ahli *is a predator in nature, happily feeding on small fish and young fry. It is often sold under the name* Haplochromis jacksoni.

Ideal conditions

pH / Hardness: 7.5-8.5 / 15-25°dGH.
Temperature: 24-26°C (75-79°F).
Food: Flake, bloodworm, pellet foods.
Stocking: Overstock the aquarium to reduce aggression. Start with less aggressive species.
Minimum tank size: 90 cm (36 in).
Environment: Clean, well-filtered water. Open swimming space, plus rock work for caves and hiding spaces.

Two of the most beautiful aquarium fish – the discus *(Symphysodon* sp.*)* and the angelfish *(Pterophyllum* sp.*)* – are found in blackwater tributaries of the Amazon. In these tributaries, humic acids and decaying vegetation produce acidic water. In some places, where discus are found, the pH level drops to below 5.0. Angelfish are more tolerant of harder water, but still prefer a neutral to slightly acidic environment. The dwarf cichlids, such as the ram *(Papiliochromis ramirezi)* and the *Apistogramma* species, come from the same general area and also prefer a low pH and hardness. Provide open swimming areas, with tall plants around the back of the aquarium for the fish to hide in.

Discus require very good water quality, and many discus-keepers use reverse osmosis water (R.O.) in their aquariums (see page 24). However, as R.O. water is virtually pure, salts and trace elements must be added to it before it can be used in the aquarium. Once this is done, either by mixing with tap water or adding a brand-name mix to R.O. water, the result is very soft water with virtually no chemical pollutants, ideal for demanding species such as discus.

The dwarf cichlids appreciate the same soft, acidic environment and often breed in the aquarium, given the correct conditions. Many of these fish have fascinating behaviors that make them excellent fish for the interested aquarist.

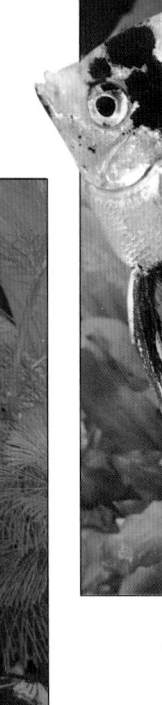

Above: *The angelfish* (Pterophyllum scalare) *is available in both wild and tank-bred forms. This is a marbled variety. With the right care and conditions, angelfish breed easily in the aquarium.*

Left: *The turquoise discus* (Symphysodon aequifasciatus haraldi) *is one of many color forms. This beautiful "king of aquarium fish" demands excellent water quality.*

Left: The coloration of the ram (Papiliochromis ramirezi) could rival that of many marine fish. Given the correct water conditions, this fish also breeds easily. Watching the fish pair off, defend a small territory, and raise young fry is a sign of competent fish husbandry and an achievement that deserves praise.

Right: A red cockatoo cichlid (Apistogramma cacatuoides), one of the color morphs of this small, relatively peaceful fish. "Whitewater" species such as this one do best over a pH range of 6.8–7.4.

Ideal conditions

pH / Hardness: 5-6.5 / 4-8°dGH.
Temperature: 26-30°C (79-86°F).
Food: Flake and live foods.
Stocking: Discus and angels: start with a school of six or more young fish. Dwarf cichlids: in pairs or 3–4 females to each male, depending on species.
Minimum tank size: 60 cm (24 in). Discus and angels, 90 cm (36 in).
Environment: Little water movement, tall plants, caves, and bogwood.

pH fluctuations

Soft, acidic water is generally harder to re-create in the aquarium than hard, alkaline water. This is because to create soft, acidic water you have to remove substances from the water, whereas with hard water you simply add them. One danger of controlling water quality in a very soft water environment is that pH fluctuations can rapidly occur. This is because in water with very low hardness, there is also very little buffering capacity (see page 25). The processes involved in waste decomposition use up the elements that create water hardness, and buffering capacity diminishes further. If this cycle continues, the water's buffering capacity will all but disappear, and the acids produced by respiration and bacterial activity will cause the pH level to drop rapidly. This drop may be enough to cause a physiological shock to the fish, strong enough to kill them. Avoid the problem by carrying out regular water changes and adding a suitable soft water pH buffer.

Most catfish are not demanding in terms of water quality and live in a range of conditions. However, grouping catfish into one category is tricky, since there are many hundreds of species. The most common groups kept in aquariums are the *Corydoras* sp. and the *Synodontis* sp., discussed below.

The corydoras group of catfish are some of the most popular fish kept in the hobby. Their small size, peaceful nature, and useful feeding habits make them ideal for virtually any fish community. In nature, they can be found in South American streams and tributaries of the Amazon River system. The water in these streams has often travelled little distance from its source. Coming from rainfall and runoff, it is still clean, clear, and unpolluted. In times of heavy rain, the streams experience an influx of cooler water and the temperature can drop quickly. The fish in these streams have adapted to the fluctuating temperatures and as a result, many corydoras can be kept in unheated aquariums. The natural substrate is usually a fine gravel bed, along which the small corydoras swim in groups, searching for small animals and food.

Although not particularly demanding in the aquarium, they do need a clean substrate. Too much waste in the substrate encourages bacteria to grow, and as the corydoras are constantly in contact with the substrate, they are easily laid open to bacterial infections. Although often sold as a good starter fish, the corydoras are not tolerant of high nitrite levels, so good water quality care and regular aquarium maintenance are essential for these fish.

The corydoras are natural scavengers and perform a useful function in the aquarium, picking up waste food matter within the substrate. However, they do need a balanced diet – as do all fish – and should be fed sinking tablet or wafer foods.

The synodontis group of catfish are found mainly in the African river systems. They, too, are scavengers searching the river bed for small animals and fallen fruits and seeds from overhanging vegetation. In the mid-reaches of the large African rivers, runoff from topsoil and forest debris lower the water's pH to as little as 6.0, and hardness often drops to nearly zero. Temperatures are also high, depending on the season. Unlike the corydoras, the synodontis can reach a formidable size, often more than 30 cm (12 in), so they are best suited to a community of larger fish. Territorial by nature, these catfish need caves and hiding places in the form of bogwood and/or rocks. Large objects in the aquarium become markers for territories, as well as places to hide from the aquarium activity.

Right: The very hardy bronze corydoras (Corydoras aeneus) *needs a smooth, rounded substrate in the aquarium, as small, sharp stones can cause damage.*

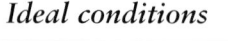

Ideal conditions

pH / Hardness: 6-8 / 5-25°dGH.
Temperature: 18-25°C (64-77°F).
Food: Sinking pellet, tablets, or wafers. Bloodworm, live foods.
Stocking: Corydoras: in schools of 3 or more. Synodontis: species dependent.
Minimum tank size: Corydoras: 45 cm (18 in); synodontis: 75 cm (30 in).
Environment: Clean, clear water, moderate current, hiding places.

The Central American cichlids are virtually all territorial and grow to a large size, so a carefully stocked, sufficiently large aquarium is essential. Provide caves and rocks, as the fish use these as territorial markers, hiding places, and breeding and spawning sites. Make sure that any rock work is firmly in place. Plants are sparse in their natural habitat and many of the cichlids happily destroy most vegetation, so include only a few hardy plants.

The water movement in the cichlids' natural habitat results in clear, well-oxygenated water. Re-create this by means of a powerful external filter. The reason for using a powerful filter, rather than just a pump, to move water is that the cichlids are very messy eaters and their size means that a lot of food waste will be entering the aquarium. An external filter, containing mechanical and biological media, will keep the water clear, clean, and well-oxygenated.

Above: *This yellow variety of the red devil cichlid* (Amphilophus labiatus) *is an aggressive, destructive fish. The red devil, like many other Central American cichlids, can adjust to a variety of pH and hardness levels, and is easy to keep in the aquarium, providing it has enough space.*

Left: *The Nicaragua cichlid* (Hypsophrys nicaraguensis) *can grow up to 25 cm (10 in) and requires a suitably large aquarium. Central American cichlids are best kept as show fish, with only a few fish in one*

Ideal conditions

pH / Hardness: 7.5-8 / 10-20°dGH.
Temperature: 24-26°C (75-79°F).
Food: Floating pellets, large frozen foods.
Stocking: Singles or pairs, depending on the size of the aquarium.
Minimum tank size: 90 cm (36 in). Larger species 120 cm (48 in).
Environment: Well-filtered and oxygenated water, open spaces, caves and hiding spots, few plants.

The rainbowfish are a beautiful group of fish that are commonly available for aquariums. Most rainbowfish do not develop their coloration until they are mature, usually at about 12 months of age. They also make ideal fish for beginners, as they are tolerant of a wide range of water conditions. This is because they are faced with widely varying water conditions in their natural habitats. Some rainbowfish come from cooler areas and appreciate the same conditions in the aquarium. It is best to try to find out about the requirements of individual species before keeping them; not all rainbowfish like the same conditions. However, generally speaking, most rainbowfish require medium-hard water and a neutral-alkaline pH. The natural environment of these fish is often well-oxygenated, so make sure that there is surface movement in the aquarium. Many rainbowfish adapt to most aquarium conditions happily, providing that the environment is well-filtered and regularly maintained.

Ideal conditions

pH / Hardness: 7-8.5 / 12-30°dGH.
Temperature: 22-25°C (72-77°F).
Food: Flake, live foods, frozen foods.
Stocking: Most rainbowfish should be kept in groups of four or more.
Minimum tank size: 60 cm (24 in).
Environment: Well-filtered and oxygenated water, dense planting in places.

Left: Boeseman's rainbowfish (Melanotaenia boesemani) *is often overlooked in retailers' aquariums, because its full and stunning coloration only develops as it ages. This is unfortunate, as this fish makes an excellent beginner's fish, able to adapt to a range of water values.*

As is the case with the rainbowfish, fish from brackish waters are accustomed to widely varying conditions in the wild, and make good aquarium subjects. These fluctuations often happen every day, but need not be re-created in the aquarium, where the aim should be to provide a stable environment. The addition of salt to the brackish aquarium creates a high hardness and pH environment that needs to be buffered and maintained by means of calcium-based additives, substrates, or rock work. The level of salinity to be achieved is debatable and depends on the needs of the fish you intend to keep and whether you wish to include a few hardy plants in the aquarium. If you intend to keep some live plants, such as *Vallisneria, Sagittaria, Microsorium,* and *Anubias,* then the salinity cannot be too high and should be kept at no more than 8gm/l. Remember to check or find out the salinity of your stockist's aquariums, so that you can take steps to acclimatize your fish to the same or similar conditions.

Above: The mono (Monodactylus argenteus) *is a peaceful, brackish water fish that should be kept in schools of six or more. In the aquarium, the fish is often timid, so provide hiding places.*

Above: The archerfish (Toxotes jaculator) *has a powerful muscle beneath a bony jaw structure that it uses to "spit" jets of water at insects resting on branches above the surface. Once hit, the insects fall into the water and become food for the fish.*

Left: Dermogenys pusillus, *a member of the halfbeak family, is found in both fresh and brackish waters. Although most halfbeaks do not reach much more than 9 cm (3.5 in) they are predatory; provide plenty of live foods.*

Ideal conditions

pH / Hardness: 8-8.5 / +30°dGH.
Temperature: 24-26°C (75-79°F).
Food: Flake, live foods, frozen foods, and cockles.
Stocking: Species dependent. Schooling fish in groups of four or more.
Minimum tank size: Species dependent: 60 cm (24 in).
Environment: Sandy or fine substrate, rocks, a few hardy plants.

A SUMMARY OF AQUARIUM CONDITIONS

Group / type of fish	pH	Hardness	Physical environment	Other considerations
Livebearers Guppies, mollies, platies, swordtails.	pH 7.0–8.5	12–30°dGH	Substrate of fine- to medium-grade gravel. Hardy plants, such as *Vallisneria* and Java fern that can tolerate harder water.	Some livebearers may benefit from salt in the tank. Many can be acclimatized to brackish water. In hard, alkaline water, most are not demanding.
Danios & barbs Zebra, giant, Bengal, leopard, and pearl danios. Arulius, striped, banded, spanner, and tinfoil barbs.	pH 6.5–7.5	7–15°dGH	Clean, clear, well-oxygenated water with good movement. Dark areas with reduced flow should also be provided.	Although constantly active in the aquarium and apparently confident, barbs and danios are, in fact, timid and easily frightened. Most are not demanding and acclimatize well.
Tetras & small barbs Cardinal, black widow, neon, phantom, silvertip, glowlight, rummy-nose, black neon tetras. Tiger, golden, cherry, checkered barbs.	pH 5.8–7.5	3–15°dGH	Dark substrate, open swimming space, combined with plants and roots. Areas of shade. Use bogwood.	Keep tetras in groups, otherwise, they lose confidence and color, and their health will suffer. Undemanding fish that thrive in most tanks. May benefit from water filtered through peat.
Gouramis & anabantids Siamese fighting fish, paradisefish, *Ctenopoma* sp., *Betta* sp., gouramis, including honey, banded, dwarf, pearl, gold, moonlight, chocolate, and kissing.	pH 6.0–7.5	5–20°dGH	Dark substrate, heavy planting, and hiding places. Use floating plants to provide cover and shade.	Oxygen levels are not important with these fish and they appreciate a lack of water movement. Provide a peaceful environment, so avoid any overactive, boisterous species. Use CO_2 as a plant fertilizer and to control pH.
Lake Malawi cichlids *Aulonacara* sp., *Copadichromis* sp., *Cynotilapia* sp., *Haplochromis* sp., *Labidochromis* sp., *Melanochromis* sp., and *Pseudotropheus* sp., among others.	pH 7.5–8.5	18–30°dGH	The back and sides of the tank should be piled with secured rock work with plenty of caves and hiding spaces. Open swimming space toward the front. Plants not necessary and likely to be destroyed.	Use calcareous rocks or substrate to maintain hardness and pH. Overstock to reduce aggression, but install powerful filtration to cope with increased waste. Do not mix with other non-Malawi fish, except certain hardy armored catfish.

Dwarf cichlids, angels, discus Rams, *Apistogramma* sp., kribensis, angelfish, discus, *Aequidens* sp.	pH 5.0–6.5 *Discus* pH 4.8–6.5	3–10°dGH	Fine, dark, lime-free substrate. Place tall plants around the back and sides of the aquarium, with open swimming spaces in the center. Use bogwood to create hiding spaces.	Like cichlids, these fish can be territorial, so do not overstock. Good water quality is essential and the use of R.O. water benefits the fish. Discus are shy; introducing some small tetras will increase their confidence.
Catfish *Corydoras* sp., *Synodontis* sp., *Hoplosternum* sp., *Ancistrus* sp., *Otocinclus* sp., *Pterygoplichthys* sp.	pH 6.0–8.0	5–25°dGH	Clean, rounded, and well-maintained substrate. Moderate current, caves, and hiding places.	Keep smaller catfish, such as *Corydoras* sp., in schools. Some of the larger *Synodontis* sp. are territorial and need large spaces with no other similar *Synodontis* species in the tank.
Central American cichlids Quetzal, Jack Dempsey, jaguar, red devil, Nicaragua, firemouth, convict, rainbow, etc.	pH 7.0–8.0	12–25°dGH	Large, secured rocks and caves. Medium- to large-grade gravel substrate, open swimming spaces. Clear, well-oxygenated water. Few very hardy plants, such as Java fern, Amazon swords and *Anubias* sp.	These cichlids are aggressive and territorial. Allow space and understock aquariums. Some species can grow large, so take care to select the right tankmates. The fish can be destructive, so any decor in the tank should be secure. Protect equipment such as heater/thermostats. Filtration should be external and heavily mechanical.
Rainbowfish Celebes rainbows, Boeseman's rainbows, New Guinea rainbow, *Melanotaenia* sp.	pH 7.0–8.5	12–30°dGH	Sand or fine gravel substrate, well-filtered and maintained water. Dense patches of vegetation.	Some rainbowfish may appreciate the addition of salt and may even be kept in brackish aquariums. The specific requirements of rainbowfish depend on the type and location of their natural habitats.
Brackish water fish Monos, scats, archerfish, mudskippers, mollies, chromides, mosquitofish, four-eyes, some gobies, and pufferfish.	pH 8.0–8.5	N/A (above 30°dGH)	Sand or fine gravel substrate, bogwood/roots to provide hiding spaces. Very few plants are suitable for brackish water, but Java fern and *Vallisneria* may survive.	Salt is needed to maintain the brackish water. Use a quarter to half the amount required for a marine aquarium and only use salt designed for aquariums. A hydrometer can be used to measure salt levels. Research the behavior of brackish fish before buying; some have territorial tendencies.

INDEX

Page numbers in **bold** indicate major entries; *italics* refer to captions and annotations; plain type indicates other text entries.

CREDITS

Practical photographs by Geoffrey Rogers
© Interpet Publishing.

The publishers would like to thank the following photographers for providing images, credited here by page number and position: B(Bottom), T(Top), C(Center), BL(Bottom Left), etc.

MP & C Piednoir/Aqua Press: 6, 27, 40, 44, 47(T), 48, 53(T), 55, 62(B), 63(TC,BR), 64(R), 65(TL,TR,B), 66(BL,T), 70
Ardea London: 60(CR)
Bruce Coleman Collection: 52(T, Jane Burton), 59(TL)
Oxford Scientific Films/www.osf.uk.com 28(C,©Mark Deeble & Victoria Stone), 51(©Science Pictures Ltd.), 61(C,©Aldo Brando Leon)
Photomax (Max Gibbs): Title page, 54(R), 58(C), 59(B), 60(BC), 61(BR), 62(C), 63(BL), 64(C), 66(BR), 67(T,B), 68(C,R), 69(T,B), 71(BL,T), 72, 73(BL,TC,TR)
Sue Scott: Copyright page, 8, 58(TR)

Artwork illustrations by Phil Holmes and Stuart Watkinson © Interpet Publishing.

The publishers would like to thank The Water Zoo, 439 Lincoln Road, Millfield, Peterborough PE1 2PE for providing space for practical photography. Thanks are also due to ComPASS (Peterborough) Ltd.; Heaver Tropics, Ash, Kent , and RossLab plc, Gravesend, Kent.